Quick Chocolate Fixes

Quick Chocolate Fixes

75 Fast and Easy Recipes for People Who Want Chocolate . . .
in a Hurry!

Leslie Weiner and
Barbara Albright

♦ ♦ ♦

Illustrations by Durell Godfrey

ST. MARTIN'S GRIFFIN

NEW YORK

*To our editor, Barbara Anderson, for her continued patience
with our fickle ways.
To Lowell and Ted, '90s kind of dads, for their
never-ending enthusiasm for taking care of their children
while we wrote this book.
To Lauren, Samantha, and Stone, our children, '90s kind of
kids, for their never-ending enthusiasm for chocolate.*

Library of Congress Cataloging-in-Publication Data

Weiner, Leslie.
    Quick chocolate fixes :   75 fast and easy recipes for people who
want chocolate . . . in a hurry / Leslie Weiner and Barbara Albright.
       p.   cm.
  ISBN 0-312-13153-4
  1. Cookery (Chocolate) 2. Quick and easy cookery. I. Albright,
Barbara. II. Title.
TX767.C5W43 1995
641.6'374—dc20   95-17390
                                                    CIP

First St. Martin's Griffin Edition: July 1995
10 9 8 7 6 5 4 3 2 1

Contents

Metric and Imperial Conversions

All of the recipes in *Quick Chocolate Fixes* were tested using U.S. Customary measuring cups and spoons. Following are approximate conversions for weight and metric measurements. Results may vary slightly when using approximate conversions. Ingredients also vary from country to country. However, we wanted to include this list so you'll be able to satisfy a chocolate craving wherever you may be.

· VOLUME CONVERSIONS ·

U.S. Customary	Approximate Metric Conversion (ml)
$\frac{1}{8}$ teaspoon	0.5 ml
$\frac{1}{4}$ teaspoon	1.0 ml
$\frac{1}{2}$ teaspoon	2.5 ml
1 teaspoon	5.0 ml
1 tablespoon (3 teaspoons)	15.0 ml
2 tablespoons	30.0 ml
3 tablespoons	45.0 ml
$\frac{1}{4}$ cup (4 tablespoons)	60.0 ml
$\frac{1}{3}$ cup ($5\frac{1}{3}$ tablespoons)	79.0 ml
$\frac{1}{2}$ cup (8 tablespoons)	118.0 ml
$\frac{2}{3}$ cup ($10\frac{2}{3}$ tablespoons)	158.0 ml
$\frac{3}{4}$ cup (12 tablespoons)	177.0 ml
1 cup	237.0 ml

· LENGTH CONVERSIONS ·

U.S. Inches	Approximate Metric Conversion (cm)
$\frac{3}{8}$ inch	Scant 1 cm
$\frac{1}{2}$ inch	1.0 cm
$\frac{5}{8}$ inch	1.5 cm
1 inch	2.5 cm
2 inches	5.0 cm
3 inches	7.5 cm
4 inches	10.0 cm
5 inches	12.5 cm
6 inches	15.0 cm
7 inches	17.5 cm
8 inches	20.0 cm
9 inches	22.5 cm
10 inches	25.0 cm
11 inches	27.5 cm
12 inches	30.0 cm
13 inches	32.5 cm
14 inches	35.0 cm
15 inches	37.5 cm

· COMMONLY USED INGREDIENT CONVERSIONS ·

ALL-PURPOSE FLOUR, UNSIFTED AND SPOONED INTO THE CUP

Volume	Ounces	Grams
¼ cup	1.1 oz	31 gm
⅓ cup	1.5 oz	42 gm
½ cup	2.2 oz	63 gm
1 cup	4.4 oz	125 gm

GRANULATED SUGAR

Volume	Ounces	Grams
1 teaspoon	.1 oz	4 gm
1 tablespoon	.4 oz	12 gm
¼ cup	1.8 oz	50 gm
⅓ cup	2.4 oz	67 gm
½ cup	3.5 oz	100 gm
1 cup	7.1 oz	200 gm

FIRMLY PACKED BROWN SUGAR

Volume	Ounces	Grams
1 tablespoon	.5 oz	14 gm
¼ cup	1.9 oz	55 gm
⅓ cup	2.6 oz	73 gm
½ cup	3.9 oz	110 gm
1 cup	7.8 oz	220 gm

Unsalted butter

Volume	Ounces	Grams
1 tablespoon	.5 oz	14 gm
1/4 cup	2.0 oz	57 gm
1/3 cup	2.6 oz	76 gm
1/2 cup	4.0 oz	113 gm
1 cup	8.0 oz	227 gm

Nuts

Volume	Ounces	Grams
1/4 cup	1.0 oz	28 gm
1/3 cup	1.3 oz	38 gm
1/2 cup	2.0 oz	57 gm
1 cup	4.0 oz	113 gm

· OVEN TEMPERATURE CONVERSIONS ·

Fahrenheit	Approximate Celsius (Centigrade)
300°F.	150°C.
325°F.	160°C.
350°F.	175°C.
375°F.	190°C.
400°F.	200°C.
425°F.	220°C.
450°F.	230°C.

Introduction

With the fairly recent arrival of our children, we've come to appreciate quick and easy recipes that deliver great taste. Since we like to tackle one subject at a time (see our list of other cookbooks opposite the title page), chocolate seemed like a natural. With more than 500 flavor components, there is hardly any other ingredient so versatile. Because of the emphasis of "quick" in this book, we've left out complicated recipes and techniques (such as tempering).

These recipes are quick to prepare, but some may take a little time for baking, freezing, or cooling. We've used chocolate chip symbols to give you a general idea of the recipe's quickness—super-super-quick, super-quick, and quick.

A whole new dimension was added to our recipe testing when our young assistants got involved. As if we weren't perfectly capable of getting confused by ourselves, mothers' little helpers created a brand-new form of kitchen chaos. When Leslie attempted to test some recipes after her daughter Lauren had gone to bed, Lauren heard the blender whirring and asked Mom if there might be some samples in store. Quick on her feet, Leslie replied that she was doing some late-night vacuuming, and Lauren bought it. Barb's daughter, Samantha, recognizes the possibility of a chocolate fix when there's any open bag of chocolate chips or a few squares of chocolate left over from a recipe. And, when she measures brown sugar, it's hard to tell whether more gets into the measuring cup or into her mouth. Both girls are impatient for each recipe to be completed, and baby Stone (Barbara's son) appreciates the chocolate treats his sister Samantha shares with him.

We hope you enjoy these quick chocolate recipes as much as have Lauren, Samantha, Stone, and our friends and neighbors.

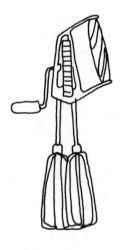

PREPARATION

Before preparing any recipe, read each one carefully and completely. Then assemble the ingredients and equipment, and prepare the pan or baking sheet, if necessary. For best results, use good-quality equipment and utensils. Measure all ingredients carefully. These simple steps will help avoid many mishaps.

Preheat the oven to the specified temperature and check the temperature of your oven with an oven thermometer. (Mercury thermometers work best.) Oven temperatures vary, however, so check baked items at the minimum baking time recommended in each recipe to avoid overbaking, especially when trying recipes for the first time. For best results, position your oven rack so that the baking pan or sheet is in the center of the oven. Test for doneness as directed in each recipe.

Follow the recipe directions for cooling baked items. This usually includes a short cooling period on a wire rack before removing the items from the baking pan or sheet to a wire rack to cool completely. If necessary, run a knife around the edges of the baked item to loosen the sides from the pan.

We do not live in a standardized world, and pan sizes are no exception. Try to stay within ¼ to ½ inch of each specified pan dimension for the best results.

MEASURING

Be sure to use the appropriate measuring cups for dry and liquid ingredients. Use measuring spoons instead of flatware. Level off measuring spoons and dry measuring cups with the flat edge of a knife. Read measurements for liquid ingredients at eye level. (Refer to individual ingredients for specific instructions.)

STORAGE

Follow the storage suggestions in each recipe. Several of the recipes, such as those using puff pastry and phyllo dough, as well as many of the beverages, should be consumed right away. Others will keep in airtight containers at room temperature, in the refrigerator, or in the freezer. We have noted the items that freeze well.

To store items in the freezer for up to one month (unless otherwise indicated in the recipe), wrap completely cooled baked goods in plastic wrap and then in aluminum foil. Store in an airtight container for the best results. Be sure to label and date the item before freezing so that you do not have any mystery packages in your freezer.

TYPES OF CHOCOLATE

Chocolate is available in many forms, all starting with cocoa beans. Each brand of chocolate varies depending on the cocoa beans used, how the beans are roasted, and how they are processed.

UNSWEETENED CHOCOLATE

After cocoa beans are processed and roasted, they are smoothly ground to form this purest form of chocolate. This chocolate imparts a rich chocolate flavor and is a common ingredient in all-American brownies. Baker's and Nestlé are the most common brands available in the United States.

BITTERSWEET, SEMISWEET, AND SWEET CHOCOLATES

Depending on the manufacturer, these are chocolates that have sugar and flavorings such as vanilla or vanillin added. Make sure to use the type of chocolate the recipe specifies. Substituting a different type can result in subtle or drastic differences in the taste and texture of the finished recipe. This chocolate tastes great as is.

Bittersweet chocolates include those made by Lindt, Perugina, Tobler, and Valrhona. These chocolates are commonly found in the candy or specialty foods sections of grocery stores. Semisweet chocolates include those made by Baker's, Hershey's, and Nestlé. A readily available form of sweet chocolate is Baker's German Sweet Chocolate.

MILK CHOCOLATE

This is America's favorite eating chocolate, though more and more people are eating dark chocolate. It is made of chocolate, milk solids, sugar, and flavorings such as vanilla or vanillin. Because it contains milk solids, it is more sensitive to heat, so be careful when melting it. There are many brands of this chocolate, including Dove, Hershey's, Lindt, Nestlé, Perugina, and Tobler.

WHITE CHOCOLATE

While we commonly refer to white confectionery coating as white "chocolate," the United States Standard of Identity does not classify this as chocolate. True white "chocolate" contains cocoa butter, a component of the cocoa bean, and it is ivory colored. It also contains milk solids, sugar, and flavorings such as vanilla or vanillin. Other confectionery coatings use vegetable fat in place of the cocoa butter and they are bright white. Because confectionery coatings contain milk solids, they are more sensitive to heat, so be careful when melting them. Lindt and Baker's both manufacture brands that are commonly available.

Chocolate Chips

Chocolate chips are the defining component of America's favorite cookie. They are also called morsels and bits. The addition of lecithin and other stabilizers helps the chips hold their shape when they are used in baked goods. Many manufacturers make chocolate chips in a variety of flavors and sizes from miniature to jumbo. When they are stirred into a cookie, brownie, or muffin recipe as is, they can usually be used interchangeably; however, because of the milk solids, milk and white chocolate chips may burn a little bit where they touch the pans.

Cocoa Powder

This easy-to-use form of chocolate is made from plain chocolate that has nearly all of the cocoa butter pressed out of it. There are basically two types of unsweetened cocoa powder: nonalkalized and alkalized (also called European-style or Dutch processed). Nonalkalized cocoa powder has a robust, true chocolate flavor and delivers a rich chocolate flavor in baked goods. Alkalized cocoa powder has been treated with an alkali to smooth out cocoa's somewhat raw flavor. It is ideally suited for use when foods are not cooked—for instance, for rolling truffles in or dusting the tops of cakes. Use the type of cocoa powder specified in the recipe because the leavening can be affected. If not specified, you can use either kind. Hershey's makes both types of cocoa powder.

Note: Specialty chocolate and cocoa powders are often available. They may include flavorings or the addition of ingredients such as nuts.

CHOCOLATE KNOW-HOW

Chocolate's one-of-a-kind flavor deserves to be treated with tender loving care. Here are some tips to help you when you are working with chocolate.

Storing Chocolate

Store chocolate in a cool (about 65°F.), dry place. Do not store it in the refrigerator or freezer unless absolutely necessary to avoid a meltdown (you have no air conditioner and there's a heat wave). Storing chocolate in a place that is too damp or too hot can cause the chocolate to develop a grayish cast (called bloom) on the surface of the chocolate. Chocolate that has bloomed is perfectly safe to eat and cook with; however, the texture of the chocolate may be affected.

Melting Chocolate

While you can melt chocolate in a double boiler on top of the stove, the microwave oven has made melting chocolate a snap. It cuts down on the risk that the chocolate will seize (become coarse-textured and clump together). This happens sometimes when steam or water comes in contact with the chocolate. Place the chocolate (broken into pieces if you are using large bars) in a microwave-safe bowl. Heat in a microwave oven on HIGH for 1 to 2 minutes, stirring halfway through cooking, until the chocolate is melted. For large amounts, continue the process, 1 minute at a time. The chocolate turns shiny as it melts. Stir the chocolate because it is probably melted even though it appears to have held its shape.

You can also melt chocolate the old-fashioned way, in the top of a double boiler. Place coarsely chopped chocolate in the top of a double boiler over hot, not simmering, water. Melt the chocolate, stirring until smooth. Remove the top of the double boiler from the bottom of the pan.

INGREDIENTS

FLOUR

Unless otherwise specified, the recipes call for all-purpose flour, as this is the type of flour that most people have on hand. To measure any type of flour, lightly spoon the flour into the appropriate dry measuring cup. Try not to be heavy-handed. Level it off with the straight edge of a knife. Do not tap the cup or dip it into the flour or you will end up with more flour than is needed.

SUGAR

We've used granulated sugar, confectioners' sugar, and brown sugar in these recipes. In addition to adding sweetness, sugar is important to the texture of baked items. Measure granulated sugar by filling the appropriate dry measuring cup(s). Level it off with the straight edge of a knife. Measure confectioners' sugar in the same way that you measure flour. Light and dark brown sugar are basically interchangeable in recipes. Dark brown sugar will produce darker baked items. To measure brown sugar, press it firmly into the appropriate-size dry measuring cup(s) until it is level with the top edge. It should hold the form of the cup when turned out.

Store brown sugar in airtight containers in a cool place. One manufacturer recommends freezing brown sugar for lengthy storage, and most manufacturers include softening directions on the package should your brown sugar become dry and rocklike. One recommended method is to place the brown sugar in an airtight plastic container, cover the surface of the sugar with a piece of plastic wrap, and top with a folded moist paper towel. Seal the container for eight to twelve hours before removing the towel.

Whether you've had to soften your brown sugar or not, we've found that it is a good idea to squeeze the brown sugar between your fingertips as you add it to the mixture to eliminate sugar clumps in the finished product.

BAKING POWDER AND BAKING SODA

These two items are not interchangeable. Use whichever is called for in the recipe. Use double-acting baking powder, which is the type most readily available. (We have noticed that a few single-acting baking powders have been sneaking onto grocers' shelves.)

Double-acting baking powder enables leavening to occur both at room temperature and during baking. It contains two acid components, calcium acid phosphate and sodium aluminum sulfate, along with an alkali component, sodium bicarbonate (baking soda), and cornstarch. Adding liquid to baking powder causes a chemical reaction between the acid and alkali, forming carbon dioxide and water. Leavening occurs when heat causes carbon dioxide gas to be released into the dough or batter.

When acid ingredients (such as buttermilk, yogurt, sour cream, citrus, cranberries, and molasses) are used in baking, it is usually necessary to add baking soda (sodium bicarbonate—an alkali) to balance the acid-alkali ratio.

Make sure your baking powder and baking soda are fresh. They can lose their potency if stored past the expiration date or if moisture gets into the container.

SALT

Our recipes use very little salt and, when divided among servings, the amount of salt is minimal. Don't leave it out. We think you will find that just a little bit greatly enhances the flavor of most baked goods.

EGGS

Select large, uncracked eggs. Letting the eggs reach room temperature before use makes it easier to incorporate them into the batter, but do not let them stand at room temperature for more than two hours. Because of the potential danger of salmonella in raw eggs, it is not advisable to taste any mixture containing uncooked eggs. Eggs should always be cooked to 160° F. to reduce the risk of salmonella.

To bring refrigerated eggs to room temperature in a hurry, submerge them in a bowl of very warm water.

BUTTER

Use unsalted (often called sweet) butter in these recipes so that you can more accurately control the amount of salt in the recipe. The recipes will taste better, too. Salt acts as a preservative and may mask the flavor of butter that is past its prime. Unsalted butter has a shorter shelf life, so if you are keeping it for long periods of time, be sure to freeze it. You may substitute unsalted margarine. However, do not substitute vegetable oil and expect to get the same results.

Vanilla Extract

Use the real thing for better-tasting results. Vanilla adds a full, rich flavor to most chocolate recipes and it often allows you to get by with a little less sugar.

Spices

Store spices in airtight containers away from light and heat. Older spices may lose their potency, so it is a good idea to date your containers at the time of purchase.

Fruits

Use the fruits called for in each recipe. For example, do not substitute chopped fresh fruit for dried fruit, and vice versa.

Peanut Butter

Use commercially prepared regular (not reduced-fat) peanut butter in our recipes. The health-food-store variety may change the texture of the recipe.

Nuts

It is a good idea to taste nuts before using them, as they can become rancid and spoil your recipes. Store nuts in airtight containers in the refrigerator or freezer. We like nuts and have used them in many recipes. If chopped nuts are supposed to be stirred into a batter or dough, you can usually leave them out if you do not care for nuts. Remember, however, that the volume will decrease if you omit the nuts.

MAIL ORDER SOURCES

Dried Cherries and Dried Cranberries:
American Spoon Foods, Inc.
1668 Clarion Avenue
P.O. Box 566
Petoskey, MI 49770-0566
(616) 347-9030 or (800) 222-5886

Dried Cherries:
Amon Orchards
7404 US 31 North
P.O. Box 1551
Traverse City, MI 49685
(616) 938-9160

Hazelnuts:
Evonuk Oregon Hazelnuts
P.O. Box 7121
Eugene, OR 97401

Baking Equipment:
Maid of Scandinavia
3244 Raleigh Avenue
Minneapolis, MN 55416
(800) 328-6722

Quick Chocolate Cakes and Quick Breads

· ALMOST FLOURLESS CHOCOLATE CAKE ·

Keep one of these cakes in your freezer so you'll always have a dessert that's ready to go. It's great served in a pool of Raspberry Sauce (page 99).

12 ounces bittersweet chocolate, coarsely broken
¾ cup (1½ sticks) unsalted butter
5 large eggs, at room temperature
⅓ cup granulated sugar

¼ cup light corn syrup
3 tablespoons all-purpose flour
2 teaspoons vanilla extract
Confectioners' sugar for dusting top of cake

1.   Preheat oven to 350°F. Lightly butter an 8-inch springform pan. Line bottom of pan with a circle of baking parchment or wax paper. Place pan on a piece of aluminum foil and press it to cover bottom and part of side to prevent any batter from leaking out.

2.   In a microwave-safe bowl, heat chocolate and butter in a microwave oven on HIGH for 1 to 3 minutes, stirring halfway through cooking, until chocolate is melted (or use a double boiler over hot, not simmering, water). Let stand at room temperature until tepid.

3.   In a large bowl, using a hand-held electric mixer, beat eggs and sugar until slightly thickened. Add corn syrup and beat until a ribbon forms when beaters are lifted. Beat in flour. Beat in vanilla. Add chocolate mixture and fold together until combined. Scrape into prepared pan. Bake for 50 to 60 minutes, or until a cake tester inserted in center comes out slightly moist.

4.   Remove pan to a wire rack. Run a thin knife around edge of pan to release cake.

Cool cake completely in pan on rack before carefully removing side of springform pan. Sift confectioners' sugar over top of cake. Cover and store cake in refrigerator.

This cake freezes well.

Makes 10 servings

· BANANA TOFFEE CRUNCH BUNDT CAKE WITH CHOCOLATE GLAZE ·

Serve this delicious cake with the suggested Chocolate Glaze or with Chocolate Sauce (page 132).

CAKE

3 cups all-purpose flour
2 teaspoons baking powder
1 teaspoon baking soda
¾ teaspoon salt
2 cups mashed ripe bananas (about 4 large)
¼ cup milk, at room temperature
2 teaspoons vanilla extract
⅔ cup (1 stick plus 2⅔ tablespoons) unsalted butter, at room temperature

1 cup granulated sugar
4 large eggs, at room temperature
5 bars (1.4 ounces each) milk chocolate-coated toffee bars, chopped
⅔ cup chopped slivered blanched almonds, toasted (see Note)

CHOCOLATE GLAZE

3 ounces semisweet chocolate
3 tablespoons unsalted butter

1. *To prepare cake:* Preheat oven to 350°F. Butter a 12-cup Bundt pan or fluted tube pan. Lightly dust with flour and tap out excess.

2. In a small bowl, stir together flour, baking powder, baking soda, and salt. In another small bowl, stir together bananas, milk, and vanilla until blended.

3. In a large bowl, using a hand-held electric mixer, cream together butter and sugar until blended. One at a time, add eggs, beating well after each addition. In three additions each, alternately beat in flour mixture and banana mixture, until just combined. Stir in toffee and nuts.

4. Scrape batter into prepared pan and spread evenly. Bake for 65 to 75 minutes, or until a cake tester inserted in center of cake comes out clean.

5. Remove pan to a wire rack. Cool for 10 minutes before inverting cake onto a cooling rack; finish cooling on rack.

6. *To prepare glaze:* In a small saucepan, melt chocolate and butter over low heat, stirring often until mixture is completely smooth, with no streaks. Remove from heat and cool for 5 minutes. Pour evenly over cooled cake. Place cake in refrigerator for 30 minutes to set glaze. Store cooled cake in an airtight container in refrigerator. Allow cake to reach room temperature before serving.

Makes 1 cake; 12 to 16 slices

Note: To toast almonds, place them in a single layer on a baking sheet and bake at 350°F. for 5 to 7 minutes, shaking sheet a couple of times, until nuts are lightly browned.

• BLACK-AND-WHITE CUPCAKES •

The combination of chocolate cake and cheesecake makes these extra special.

TOPPING

8 ounces cream cheese, at room
   temperature
²/₃ cup confectioners' sugar

1 large egg, at room temperature
2 tablespoons all-purpose flour
1 teaspoon vanilla extract

CUPCAKES

6 ounces bittersweet chocolate, chopped
¹/₄ cup unsalted butter
¹/₂ cup buttermilk, at room temperature
1 large egg, at room temperature
1¹/₂ teaspoons vanilla extract

1 cup all-purpose flour
¹/₂ cup granulated sugar
¹/₂ teaspoon baking soda
¹/₄ teaspoon salt
¹/₂ cup miniature semisweet chocolate chips

1.   Preheat oven to 375°F. Lightly butter twelve 3 × 1¹/₄-inch (3¹/₂- to 4-ounce)
muffin cups.

2.   *To prepare topping:* In a small bowl, whisk together all ingredients until smooth.
Set aside.

3.   *To prepare cupcakes:* In a small heavy saucepan, over low heat, stir chocolate and
butter until melted. Cool for 10 minutes. In a medium bowl, stir together buttermilk,
egg, and vanilla until blended. Stir in chocolate mixture. In a large bowl, stir together

flour, sugar, baking soda, and salt. Make a well in center of flour mixture; add chocolate mixture and stir just to combine. Stir in chips.

4. Place a heaping tablespoonful of batter in bottom of each cup, using no more than half of chocolate batter. Divide the cream cheese topping among muffin cups. (Each cup will contain a generous tablespoonful.) Divide remaining chocolate batter among muffin cups (approximately 1 level tablespoon of batter in each cup). Bake for 20 to 30 minutes, or until a cake tester comes out clean. Do not overbake. Remove muffin tin(s) to a wire rack. Cool for 5 minutes before removing the muffins from cups; finish cooling on rack. Store completely cooled muffins in an airtight container in refrigerator. Let cupcakes reach room temperature before serving.

Makes 12 cupcakes

• BROWNIE CHEESECAKE •

Here's a dessert to make ahead for your next dinner party. A brownie base is topped with a cream cheese mixture swirled with chocolate for a finale sure to garner rave reviews.

3 ounces semisweet chocolate
2 ounces unsweetened chocolate
2 packages (8 ounces each) cream cheese,
  at room temperature
1⅓ cups granulated sugar, divided
3 large eggs, at room temperature,
  divided

2 teaspoons vanilla extract, divided
½ cup (1 stick) unsalted butter, at room
  temperature
½ cup all-purpose flour
¼ teaspoon salt

1. Preheat oven to 350°F. Lightly butter bottom and side of an 8-inch springform pan. Place pan on a piece of aluminum foil and press it to cover bottom and part of side to prevent any batter from leaking out.

2. In a microwave-safe bowl, heat chocolates in microwave oven on HIGH for 1 to 3 minutes, stirring halfway through cooking, until chocolate is melted (or use a double boiler over hot, not simmering, water). Let stand at room temperature for 10 minutes.

3. *To prepare cream cheese topping:* In a large bowl, using a hand-held electric mixer set at medium speed, beat together cream cheese and ⅓ cup of the sugar until smooth. Beat in 1 of the eggs and 1 teaspoon of the vanilla until combined. Set aside.

4. *To prepare chocolate batter:* In another large bowl, using a hand-held electric mixer

set at medium speed, beat together butter and remaining 1 cup of sugar until combined. One at a time, beat in remaining 2 eggs, beating well after each addition. Beat in melted chocolate and remaining 1 teaspoon vanilla. On low speed, beat in flour and salt until just combined.

5. Scrape all but ½ cup of chocolate batter into prepared pan and smooth surface. Spread cream cheese topping evenly over chocolate batter. Spoon reserved chocolate batter over cream cheese topping. Pull a table knife or a small metal spatula through layers of batter in a zigzag fashion to create a marbled effect. Bake for 50 to 60 minutes, or until a cake tester inserted 2 inches from center comes out slightly moist.

6. Remove pan to wire rack. Run a thin knife around edge of pan to release cheesecake. (This step will help to prevent cheesecake from cracking as it cools.) Cool cake for 1 to 2 hours before carefully removing side of springform pan. Or, cover top of springform pan tightly with plastic wrap and refrigerate cheesecake until about 30 minutes before serving. Cover and store cake in refrigerator.

Makes 12 servings

• CHOCOLATE CHOCOLATE CHIP CHEESECAKE •

A super-rich dessert for extra-special occasions. Cream-filled chocolate sandwich cookies make an extra-decadent crust.

COOKIE CRUST
15 cream-filled chocolate sandwich cookies, crushed into crumbs

2 tablespoons unsalted butter, melted and cooled

CHEESE FILLING
2 packages (8 ounces each) cream cheese, at room temperature
1 cup firmly packed light brown sugar
3 large eggs, at room temperature
1/2 cup sour cream, at room temperature

1 teaspoon vanilla extract
8 ounces bittersweet chocolate, melted and cooled
3 tablespoons all-purpose flour
3/4 cup miniature semisweet chocolate chips

1. Preheat oven to 325°F. Lightly butter side of an 8-inch springform pan. Place pan on a double-thick piece of aluminum foil and press it to cover bottom and part of side to prevent any melted butter from leaking out.

2. *To prepare crust:* Mix together cookie crumbs and butter. Press into bottom and 3/4 inch up side of prepared pan. Place in freezer.

3. *To prepare filling:* In a large bowl, using a hand-held electric mixer set at low speed, beat cheese until soft. Beat in sugar until blended. One at a time, add eggs, beating well with a fork after each addition. Using a fork, beat in sour cream and vanilla,

until combined. Beat in bittersweet chocolate until blended. Stir in flour until blended. Stir in chocolate chips. Scrape batter into pan. Bake for 75 to 90 minutes, or until a cake tester inserted 1 inch from center comes out almost clean. Leave pan in oven with door partially open for 30 minutes. Remove pan to a wire rack to cool to room temperature, no more than 2 hours. Refrigerate for 6 hours, or until chilled. To serve, run a metal spatula around edge. Release side. Let sit at room temperature for 10 minutes before serving.

Makes 8 to 10 servings

Note: This cake may sink and crack slightly while cooling, but the results are still delicious.

· CHOCOLATE CHUNK SCONES ·

Warm from the oven, the chocolate chunks in these scones are meltingly delicious. For more traditional scones, substitute ½ cup of raisins or currants for the chocolate chunks.

2 large eggs, lightly beaten, divided
½ cup buttermilk
1½ teaspoons vanilla extract
2 cups all-purpose flour
⅓ cup granulated sugar
1½ teaspoons baking powder
½ teaspoon baking soda

¼ teaspoon salt
⅓ cup unsalted butter, chilled and cut into
 ½-inch chunks
6 ounces milk, bittersweet, or German sweet
 chocolate, cut into ½-inch chunks
⅓ cup coarsely broken walnuts

1. Preheat oven to 400°F. Lightly butter a baking sheet.
2. Reserve 1 tablespoon of egg for brushing on top of scones. In a medium bowl, stir together buttermilk, remaining eggs, and vanilla.
3. In a large bowl, stir together flour, sugar, baking powder, baking soda, and salt. Distribute butter chunks over flour mixture. With fingertips, quickly rub butter into flour mixture until mixture resembles coarse crumbs. Stir buttermilk mixture into flour mixture until combined. Stir in chocolate chunks and walnuts.
4. Turn dough out onto a lightly floured surface and knead until combined, about 30 to 60 seconds. With lightly floured hands, pat dough into a 9-inch-diameter circle on prepared baking sheet. Brush reserved egg over top and side of dough. With serrated

knife, cut into 8 wedges. Bake for 14 to 17 minutes, or until lightly browned and a cake tester inserted in center of a scone comes out clean.

5. Remove baking sheet to a wire rack and cool for 5 minutes. Using a metal spatula, transfer scones to wire rack and cool for about 10 minutes. Recut into wedges, if necessary. Scones are best served warm.

Makes 8 scones

· CHOCOLATE COFFEE CAKE ·

Here's a cake you'll want to serve warm from the oven at your next breakfast or brunch.

CHOCOLATE CHIP STREUSEL MIXTURE

1/3 cup all-purpose flour
1/4 cup firmly packed brown sugar
1/8 teaspoon ground cinnamon (optional)
3 tablespoons unsalted butter, chilled and
  cut into 1/2-inch cubes

1/3 cup miniature semisweet chocolate chips
1/3 cup chopped walnuts or pecans

CHOCOLATE COFFEE CAKE

2 cups all-purpose flour
1/2 cup unsweetened, nonalkalized cocoa
  powder
1 teaspoon baking powder
1/2 teaspoon baking soda
1/4 teaspoon salt
1/2 cup (1 stick) unsalted butter, at room
  temperature

1 cup granulated sugar
2 large eggs, at room temperature
1 teaspoon vanilla extract
1 1/3 cups buttermilk, at room temperature
2/3 cup miniature semisweet chocolate chips

1. Preheat oven to 350°F. Lightly butter a 9-inch-square baking pan.
2. *To prepare chocolate chip streusel mixture:* In a small bowl, stir together flour, brown sugar, and cinnamon, if desired. Distribute butter chunks evenly over flour mixture.

With a pastry blender or two knives used scissors fashion, cut in butter until mixture resembles coarse crumbs. Stir in chips and nuts. Set aside.

3. *To prepare chocolate coffee cake:* In a medium bowl, stir together flour, cocoa powder, baking powder, baking soda, and salt. In another bowl, using a hand-held electric mixer set at medium-high speed, cream together butter and sugar until blended. One at a time, add eggs, beating well after each addition. Beat in vanilla. In three additions each, alternately beat in flour mixture and buttermilk, beating just until combined. Stir in chips.

4. Scrape half the batter into prepared pan and spread evenly. Sprinkle surface evenly with half the streusel mixture. Top with remaining batter and spread evenly. Sprinkle with remaining streusel mixture.

5. Bake for 45 to 55 minutes, or until a cake tester inserted in center of cake comes out clean.

6. Remove pan to a wire rack. Cut into squares to serve. Serve warm or at room temperature. Store in an airtight container at cool room temperature.

Makes 9 servings

· CHOCOLATE MALT CUPCAKES ·

Reminiscent of a malted milk shake, these cupcakes are great at kids' birthday parties.

CUPCAKES

1²/₃ cups all-purpose flour
²/₃ cup malted milk powder (original flavor)
½ cup granulated sugar
¼ cup firmly packed light brown sugar
2 teaspoons baking powder

¼ teaspoon salt
½ cup milk
⅓ cup unsalted butter, melted and cooled
2 large eggs, at room temperature
1 teaspoon vanilla extract
²/₃ cup miniature semisweet chocolate chips

TOPPING

½ cup heavy (whipping) cream
⅓ cup malted milk powder (original flavor)
¾ cup semisweet chocolate chips, melted and cooled

12 chocolate-coated malted milk balls, for garnish (optional)

1. Preheat oven to 375°F. Lightly butter twelve 3 × 1¼-inch (3½- to 4-ounce) muffin cups.

2. *To prepare cupcakes:* In a large bowl, stir together flour, malted milk powder, sugars, baking powder, and salt. In another bowl, stir together milk, butter, eggs, and

vanilla until blended. Make a well in center of flour mixture; add milk mixture and stir just to combine. Stir in chips.

3.   Spoon batter into prepared muffin cups; bake for 20 to 25 minutes, or until a cake tester inserted in center of one cupcake comes out clean.

4.   Remove muffin tin(s) to a wire rack. Cool for 5 minutes before removing cupcakes from cups; finish cooling on rack.

5.   *To prepare topping:* In chilled bowl and with chilled beaters, beat cream and malted milk powder until stiff peaks form. Beat in melted chocolate. Chill until firm enough to spread.

6.   Divide topping among cupcakes and spread to coat tops evenly. Garnish each with a malted milk ball, if desired.

Makes 12 cupcakes

· CHOCOLATE SOUR CREAM POUND CAKE ·

Here's a cake that is great for snacks. It can also become the luscious ingredient in other recipes (like Chocolate Tiramisù, page 85). Try topping a slice with a scoop of ice cream and a drizzle of Chocolate Sauce (page 132) for a decadent dessert.

2½ cups all-purpose flour
¾ cup unsweetened, nonalkalized cocoa
    powder
½ teaspoon baking powder
½ teaspoon baking soda
½ teaspoon salt
1 cup (2 sticks) unsalted butter, at room
    temperature

2 cups granulated sugar
4 large eggs, at room temperature
1 tablespoon vanilla extract
1 cup sour cream, at room temperature
Confectioners' sugar for dusting top of cake
    (optional)

1. Preheat oven to 325°F. Lightly butter a 12-cup Bundt pan or fluted tube pan. Lightly dust with flour and tap out excess.

2. In a large bowl, stir together flour, cocoa powder, baking powder, baking soda, and salt. In another large bowl, using a hand-held electric mixer, beat together butter and sugar until combined. One at a time, beat in eggs, beating well after each addition. Beat in vanilla. In three additions each, beat in flour mixture and sour cream, beating until just combined.

3. Scrape batter into prepared pan and spread evenly. Bake for 60 to 70 minutes, or until a cake tester inserted in center of cake comes out clean.

4. Remove pan to a wire rack and cool for 10 minutes. Carefully invert cake onto rack and cool completely. Dust top of cake with confectioners' sugar, if desired. Store completely cooled cake in an airtight container at cool room temperature.

This cake freezes well.

Makes 16 to 20 servings

· EASY CHOCOLATE BIRTHDAY CAKE ·

If you want the base of your cake to be neat and tidy, before you frost it tuck strips of wax paper (each about 2 inches wide) under the bottom edge of the cake so that the entire perimeter of the cake is surrounded by the wax paper strips. After you finish frosting the cake, carefully remove the strips of wax paper.

BETTER-THAN-JUST-BASIC CHOCOLATE CAKE

2 cups all-purpose flour
2½ teaspoons baking powder
¼ teaspoon salt
½ cup (1 stick) unsalted butter, at room temperature
¼ cup vegetable oil

1½ cups granulated sugar
5 ounces unsweetened chocolate, melted and cooled
2½ teaspoons vanilla extract
3 large eggs, at room temperature
1⅓ cups milk, at room temperature

FLUFFY CHOCOLATE FROSTING

½ cup (1 stick) unsalted butter, at room temperature
2 ounces unsweetened chocolate, melted and cooled

3 cups confectioners' sugar
1 teaspoon vanilla extract
1 to 4 tablespoons milk

1.   *To prepare cake:* Preheat oven to 350°F. Lightly butter bottoms and sides of two 9-inch round cake pans. Line bottoms of pans with circles of baking parchment or wax paper. Dust sides of pans with flour and tap out excess.

2. In a medium bowl, stir together flour, baking powder, and salt.

3. In a large bowl, using a hand-held electric mixer set at medium-high speed, beat together butter, oil, and sugar until combined. Beat in melted chocolate and vanilla. One at a time, add eggs, beating well after each addition. In three additions each, beat in flour mixture and milk, beating just until combined.

4. Divide batter between prepared pans and spread evenly. Bake for 25 to 30 minutes, or until a cake tester inserted in center of cake comes out clean.

5. Remove pans to wire racks. Cool for 10 minutes. Carefully invert cake layers onto racks and cool completely.

6. *To prepare frosting:* In a large bowl, using a hand-held electric mixer set at medium-high speed, beat butter until creamy. Beat in chocolate. With mixer set at low speed, gradually sift sugar into bowl and combine. Beat in vanilla. Beat in just enough milk to make frosting spreadable.

7. *To assemble cake:* Place one cake layer on a serving plate and spread with a layer of frosting. Top with second cake layer. Frost top and side of cake. If desired, reserve some frosting to decorate cake. Place it in a pastry bag fitted with a star tip and, squeezing gently, place frosting "stars" around edge of cake or in other desired pattern. Cover cake and store in refrigerator. Allow cake to come to room temperature before serving.

Makes 12 servings

• HAZELNUT–CHOCOLATE CHUNK BANANA MUFFINS •

Chopped-up hazelnut-chocolate bars make a delectable addition to banana muffins. Of course you can use other nut-and-chocolate bar combinations.

2 cups all-purpose flour
1½ teaspoons baking powder
¼ teaspoon baking soda
¼ teaspoon salt
½ cup unsalted butter, at room temperature
½ cup granulated sugar

2 large eggs, at room temperature
1 cup mashed ripe bananas (about 3 medium bananas)
⅓ cup milk, at room temperature
1½ teaspoons vanilla extract
9 ounces bittersweet chocolate with chopped hazelnuts, cut into ½-inch pieces

1. Preheat oven to 375°F. Lightly butter twelve 2¾ × 1⅛-inch (3-ounce) muffin cups and the edges surrounding the cups.

2. In a large bowl, stir together flour, baking powder, baking soda, and salt. In another bowl, using a hand-held electric mixer, cream butter and sugar for 1 to 2 minutes, until light and fluffy. Beat in eggs. Stir in bananas, milk, and vanilla. (The mixture will look curdled.) Add flour mixture and stir just to combine. Stir in chocolate chunks.

3. Spoon batter into prepared muffin cups; bake for 20 to 25 minutes, or until a cake tester inserted in center of one muffin comes out clean.

4. Remove muffin tin(s) to wire rack. Cool for 5 minutes before removing muffins

from tin(s); finish cooling on rack. Serve warm, or cool completely and store in an airtight container at room temperature.

These muffins freeze well.

Makes 12 muffins

· MINI TRIPLE-CHIP QUICK BREADS ·

Packed with three kinds of chocolate chips, these tiny quick breads are perfect for brunch. They are also a super lunchbox addition.

2 cups all-purpose flour
1/2 cup granulated sugar
2 teaspoons baking powder
1/2 teaspoon salt
2/3 cup milk, at room temperature
1/2 cup unsalted butter, melted and cooled

2 large eggs (at room temperature), lightly
  beaten
2 teaspoons vanilla extract
2/3 cup semisweet chocolate chips
2/3 cup milk chocolate chips
2/3 cup white chocolate chips

1. Preheat oven to 375°F. Butter six 4½ × 2½ × 1½-inch loaf pans.

2. In a large bowl, stir together flour, sugar, baking powder, and salt. In another bowl, stir together milk, butter, eggs, and vanilla until blended. Make a well in center of flour mixture; add milk mixture and stir just to combine. Stir in all chips.

3. Spoon batter into prepared pans and spread evenly. Bake for 25 to 30 minutes, or until a cake tester inserted in center of one bread comes out clean.

4. Remove pans to a wire rack. Cool for 10 minutes before removing breads from pans; finish cooling on rack. Store completely cooled loaves in an airtight container at room temperature.

These breads freeze well.

Makes 6 loaves; 6 servings

· ORANGE CHOCOLATE MUFFINS WITH WHITE CHOCOLATE CHIPS ·

Freshly grated orange zest adds just the right amount of tartness to balance the sweetness of the white chocolate chips. You can also use another kind of chip (milk chocolate or semisweet chocolate, for example), if you prefer.

½ cup (1 stick) unsalted butter
½ teaspoon grated orange peel
1¾ cups all-purpose flour
¾ cup granulated sugar
½ cup unsweetened, nonalkalized cocoa powder
2 teaspoons baking powder
¼ teaspoon baking soda

½ teaspoon salt
1 cup milk, at room temperature
1 large egg, at room temperature, lightly beaten
1 teaspoon vanilla extract
1½ cups white chocolate chips, divided

1. Preheat oven to 375°F. Lightly butter twelve 2¾ × 1⅛-inch (3-ounce) muffin cups and edges around cups.

2. In a microwave-safe bowl, heat butter and orange peel in a microwave oven on HIGH for 30 to 60 seconds, or until butter is melted.

3. In another large bowl, stir together flour, sugar, cocoa powder, baking powder, baking soda, and salt. Stir milk, egg, and vanilla into melted butter mixture until blended. Make a well in center of dry ingredients. Add liquid ingredients and stir just to combine. Stir in half of chips.

4. Spoon batter into prepared muffin cups. Sprinkle remaining chips evenly over tops of muffins. Bake for 20 to 25 minutes, or until a cake tester inserted in center of one muffin comes out clean.

5. Remove muffin tin(s) to wire rack. Cool for 5 minutes before removing muffins from tin(s); finish cooling on rack. Serve warm, or cool completely and store in an airtight container at room temperature.

Makes 12 muffins

Quick Chocolate Cookies

· BROWNIE DROPS WITH PEANUT BUTTER CHIPS ·

Peanut butter and chocolate are the perfect combination for these chewy, brownie-like cookies.

9 ounces bittersweet chocolate, broken
    into pieces
2 tablespoons unsalted butter
½ cup all-purpose flour
¼ teaspoon baking powder
⅛ teaspoon salt

⅔ cup granulated sugar
2 large eggs, at room temperature
1 teaspoon vanilla extract
¾ cup peanut butter–flavored chips
⅓ cup semisweet chocolate chips

    1. In a microwave-safe bowl, heat bittersweet chocolate and butter in a microwave oven on HIGH for 1 to 3 minutes, stirring halfway through cooking, until melted. Cool chocolate mixture for 10 minutes. (Or in top of a double boiler, over hot, not simmering, water, heat bittersweet chocolate and butter, stirring until smooth. Remove top part of double boiler from bottom and cool chocolate mixture for 10 minutes.)

    2. In a small bowl, stir together flour, baking powder, and salt. In a large bowl, using a hand-held electric mixer set at high speed, beat sugar and eggs for 3 minutes, or until mixture is light and fluffy. Gradually beat in cooled chocolate mixture. Beat in vanilla. Stir in flour mixture until combined. Stir in chips. Cover and refrigerate dough for 1 to 2 hours, or until firm enough to shape into balls. If mixture gets too firm, let stand for a few minutes at room temperature until it can be shaped.

3. Preheat oven to 350°F. Lightly butter 2 large baking sheets or line sheets with baking parchment.

4. Shape level tablespoonfuls of dough into balls. Place balls on prepared baking sheets, leaving about 2 inches between cookies. Flatten slightly. Bake one sheet at a time, for 11 to 16 minutes, or until tops of cookies are just dry and centers are still very moist. Do not overbake.

5. Remove baking sheet to a wire rack and cool for about 3 minutes. Using a metal spatula, transfer cookies to wire racks and cool completely. Store cooled cookies in an airtight container.

These cookies freeze well.

Makes approximately 34 cookies

· CHOCOLATE CHUNK OATIES ·

These jumbo-sized cookies are perfect tucked inside a lunchbox. Experiment with your favorite types of chocolate chunks and chips.

1½ cups uncooked old-fashioned rolled oats
1½ cups all-purpose flour
1 teaspoon baking powder
½ teaspoon salt
1 cup (2 sticks) unsalted butter, at room temperature

1 cup granulated sugar
3 large eggs, at room temperature
1 tablespoon vanilla extract
12 ounces bittersweet or semisweet chocolate, cut into ½-inch pieces
1 cup chopped walnuts

1. Preheat oven to 350°F. Lightly butter several baking sheets.

2. In a large bowl, stir together oats, flour, baking powder, and salt. In another bowl, using a wooden spoon, cream together butter and sugar. One at a time, add eggs, stirring well after each addition. Stir in vanilla. Gradually stir in oat mixture until combined. Stir in chocolate and nuts.

3. Using a ¼ -cup measuring cup, drop dough onto prepared baking sheets, leaving about 3 inches between cookies. Bake for 15 to 20 minutes, or until cookies are lightly browned. Remove baking sheet to a wire rack and cool for about 5 minutes. Using a metal spatula, transfer cookies to wire racks and cool completely. Repeat until all dough is used. Store cookies in an airtight container at room temperature.

These cookies freeze well.

Makes approximately 20 cookies

· CHOCOLATE COOKIES WITH PEANUT BUTTER M&M'S ·

These cookies are extra easy because cocoa powder adds chocolate flavor without the hassle of melting chocolate in the microwave or in a double boiler. Try using Reese's Pieces, regular M&M's, chocolate chips, or chocolate chunks in place of the peanut butter M&M's, or omit the stir-ins altogether for a terrific chocolate cookie.

3/4 cup unsalted butter
2/3 cup unsweetened nonalkalized cocoa powder
1 cup firmly packed brown sugar
2 cups all-purpose flour
1 teaspoon baking powder

1 teaspoon baking soda
1/4 teaspoon salt
2 large eggs, at room temperature, lightly beaten
2 teaspoons vanilla extract
1 cup peanut butter M&M's

1. Preheat oven to 350°F. Lightly butter several baking sheets.
2. In a large microwave-safe bowl, heat butter in a microwave oven on **HIGH** for 30 to 60 seconds, or until melted. Whisk in cocoa powder until combined. Whisk in brown sugar. Let mixture cool for about 5 minutes.
3. In another large bowl, stir together flour, baking powder, baking soda, and salt.
4. Whisk eggs and vanilla into butter mixture to combine. Using a wooden spoon, gradually stir in flour mixture until combined. Stir in peanut butter M&M's.
5. Drop dough by heaping tablespoonfuls (each cookie should contain about 2

tablespoons of dough) onto prepared baking sheets, leaving about 2 inches between cookies. Bake one sheet at a time, for 10 to 15 minutes, or until cookies are set; do not overbake. Remove baking sheet to a wire rack and cool for about 5 minutes. Using a metal spatula, transfer cookies to wire racks and cool completely. Repeat until all dough is used. Store cookies in an airtight container at room temperature.

These cookies freeze well.

Makes approximately 24 cookies

· CHOCOLATE SHORTBREAD ·

Meltingly rich and buttery shortbread is even more sublime when flavored with chocolate. This wedge-shaped cookie looks lovely dusted with confectioners' sugar and drizzled with melted chocolate.

½ cup (1 stick) unsalted butter, at room temperature
½ cup confectioners' sugar
1 teaspoon vanilla extract
¼ teaspoon salt
1 ounce unsweetened chocolate, melted and cooled

1 cup all-purpose flour
Additional confectioners' sugar for sprinkling on top of shortbread (optional)

1. Preheat oven to 350°F.
2. In a large bowl, using a hand-held electric mixer set on medium-high speed, beat together butter and sugar for about 2 minutes, or until light and fluffy. Beat in vanilla and salt. Beat in melted chocolate until combined.
3. Using a wooden spoon, stir in flour, just until combined.
4. Shape dough into a disk and place it between two large pieces of wax paper. Using a rolling pin, roll out dough until it forms a circle approximately 9 inches in diameter. (If dough is too soft, place it in refrigerator or freezer for 5 to 10 minutes.) Remove top sheet of wax paper. Using a plate that is slightly smaller than circle of dough as a guide, with a sharp knife, trim off and discard (or eat!) the uneven edge of dough.

5. Invert circle of dough onto ungreased baking sheet. With tines of a fork, form decorative border around outside edge of circle. Using a sharp knife or pizza cutter, cut circle into 8 or 12 wedges. Bake for 15 to 18 minutes, or until shortbread is just starting to brown around edge. Transfer baking sheet to a wire rack and cool for 10 minutes. Recut into wedges, if necessary. Transfer shortbread to a wire rack and cool completely. If desired, dust top of shortbread with confectioners' sugar. Store completely cooled shortbread in an airtight container at cool room temperature.

These cookies freeze well.

Makes 8 to 12 cookies

For Shortbread with Nuts: After stirring in flour, stir in 1 cup of finely chopped nuts such as walnuts, hazelnuts, pecans, almonds, macadamia nuts, or pistachios. Proceed as directed.

For Shortbread with Chocolate Chips: After stirring in flour, stir in ½ cup miniature semisweet chocolate chips. The chips can be combined with 1 cup finely chopped nuts as well. Proceed as directed.

For Chocolate-Drizzled Hearts: After rolling out dough, using a heart-shaped cookie cutter, cut out cookies. Transfer dough hearts to baking sheet. Repeat the procedure with remaining chilled dough. Press together dough scraps and chill, if necessary, before rerolling; continue until all dough is used.

Place 1 ounce of semisweet or bittersweet chocolate in bottom corner of a small, freezer-weight zipper-style plastic storage bag. Seal bag. Microwave on HIGH for 1 to 2 minutes, or until chocolate is melted. Fold down top of bag and snip off a tiny piece of bottom corner, leaving an opening that is about ⅛ inch in diameter. Holding top of bag tightly, drizzle chocolate over cookies. The yield will vary depending on size of cookie cutter.

· CRANBERRY ORANGE WHITE CHOCOLATE OATIES ·

The tangy combination of cranberry and white chocolate creates unique and unforgettable oatmeal cookies.

1⅓ cups all-purpose flour
1 teaspoon baking powder
¼ teaspoon salt
¾ cup plus 2 tablespoons (1¾ sticks)
    unsalted butter, at room temperature
1 cup firmly packed light brown sugar
1 large egg, at room temperature

1 teaspoon vanilla extract
¾ teaspoon grated orange peel
2¼ cups uncooked old-fashioned rolled oats
3 ounces white chocolate, cut into chunks
⅔ cup dried cranberries (see Note)
½ cup chopped walnuts or pecans

1. Preheat oven to 350°F. Lightly butter several baking sheets or line sheets with baking parchment.

2. In a small bowl, stir together flour, baking powder, and salt. In a large bowl, using a wooden spoon, cream together butter and sugar until combined. Stir in egg, vanilla, and orange peel until blended. Gradually stir in flour mixture until combined. Stir in oats. Stir in chocolate, cranberries, and nuts.

3. Shape rounded tablespoonfuls of dough into balls. Place balls on prepared baking sheets, leaving about 2 inches between cookies. Flatten slightly. Bake one sheet at a time, for 12 to 17 minutes, or until bottoms of cookies are lightly browned. Remove baking sheet to a wire rack and cool for about 2 minutes. Using a metal spatula, transfer

cookies to wire racks and cool completely. Repeat until all cookies are baked. Store cookies in an airtight container at room temperature.

Makes approximately 40 cookies

Note: Dried cranberries are often available in gourmet stores, or can be ordered by mail (page 12).

· KISS-TOPPED CHOCOLATE-SPECKLED PEANUT BUTTER COOKIES ·

Miniature chocolate chips stud chewy peanut butter cookies that are sealed with a kiss— a chocolate one, that is.

⅔ cup smooth peanut butter
¼ cup (½ stick) unsalted butter, at room temperature
1 cup firmly packed brown sugar
2 large eggs, at room temperature

2 teaspoons vanilla extract
1½ cups all-purpose flour
¼ teaspoon salt
1½ cups miniature semisweet chocolate chips
About 45 Hershey's Kisses, unwrapped

1. Preheat oven to 350°F.
2. In a large bowl, using a hand-held electric mixer set at medium speed, beat together peanut butter, butter, and sugar until combined. One at a time, add eggs, beating well after each addition. Beat in vanilla. On low speed, beat in flour and salt just until combined. Stir in chips.
3. Shape dough into 1-inch balls and place on ungreased baking sheet, leaving about 2 inches between cookies. Bake for 12 to 15 minutes, or until lightly browned. Remove cookies from oven and immediately press an unwrapped Kiss into the top of each cookie, pressing down so that cookie cracks a little bit around the edge. Using a metal spatula, transfer cookies to wire racks and cool completely. Repeat until all dough is used. When cool, store cookies in an airtight container.

Makes approximately 45 cookies

· ORANGE CHOCOLATE CHIP COOKIES ·

A classic combination of chocolate and orange.

1½ cups all-purpose flour
¾ teaspoon baking powder
¼ teaspoon salt
½ cup (1 stick) unsalted butter, at room
temperature

¾ cup firmly packed light brown sugar
1 large egg, at room temperature
1 teaspoon vanilla extract
½ teaspoon grated orange peel
¾ cup miniature semisweet chocolate chips

1. In a large bowl, stir together flour, baking powder, and salt. In another bowl, using a wooden spoon, cream together butter and sugar until combined. Stir in egg until blended. Stir in vanilla and orange peel. Stir in flour mixture until combined. Stir in chips. Cover and refrigerate dough for 1 hour.

2. Preheat oven to 350°F. Lightly butter three large baking sheets or line sheets with baking parchment.

3. Drop dough by level tablespoonfuls onto prepared baking sheets, leaving about 2 inches between cookies. Flatten slightly, if desired. Bake one sheet at a time, for 10 to 15 minutes, or until bottoms of cookies are lightly browned. Remove baking sheet to a wire rack and cool for about 3 minutes. Using a metal spatula, transfer cookies to wire racks and cool completely. Repeat until all dough is used. When cool, store cookies in an airtight container.

Makes approximately 27 cookies

· THE CHOCOLATIEST CHOCOLATE CHUNK COOKIES ·

When you are looking for an intense chocolate cookie experience, these are the cookies to satisfy that craving.

2¹/₂ cups all-purpose flour
1¹/₂ teaspoons baking powder
¹/₂ teaspoon salt
1 cup (2 sticks) unsalted butter, at room temperature
1¹/₂ cups granulated sugar
3 large eggs, at room temperature

4 ounces unsweetened chocolate, melted and cooled
2 teaspoons vanilla extract
15 ounces bittersweet chocolate, cut into ¹/₂-inch pieces
1 cup broken walnuts or pecans

1. Preheat oven to 325°F.
2. In a large bowl, stir together flour, baking powder, and salt. In another bowl, using a wooden spoon, cream together butter and sugar until combined. One at a time, add eggs, stirring well after each addition. Stir in melted chocolate and vanilla. Gradually stir in flour mixture until combined. Stir in chocolate chunks and nuts.
3. Drop dough by heaping tablespoonfuls (each cookie should contain about 2 tablespoons of dough) onto ungreased baking sheet, leaving at least 2 inches between cookies. Bake one sheet at a time, for 17 to 20 minutes, or until cookies are set. Remove baking sheet to a wire rack and cool for 5 minutes. Using a metal spatula, transfer cookies

to wire racks and cool completely. Repeat until all dough is used. When cool, store cookies in an airtight container.

These cookies freeze well.

Makes approximately 45 cookies

· TOASTED ALMOND MOCHA CHIP COOKIES ·

Flavored with mocha and toasted almonds, these are a grown-up version of the classic chocolate chip cookie.

1 1/3 cups all-purpose flour (see Note)
1/2 teaspoon baking powder
1/4 teaspoon salt
1/2 cup (1 stick) unsalted butter, at room temperature
3/4 cup firmly packed light brown sugar
1 large egg, at room temperature
1 teaspoon vanilla extract

1/2 to 1 teaspoon instant espresso powder (see Note)
3 ounces coffee-flavored Swiss milk chocolate, cut into approximately 1/4-inch squares
2 ounces bittersweet chocolate, coarsely chopped
1/3 cup slivered blanched almonds, toasted (see Note)

1.   In a small bowl, stir together flour, baking powder, and salt. In a large bowl, using a wooden spoon, cream together butter and sugar until combined. Stir in egg until blended. In a small bowl or cup, stir together vanilla and espresso powder, until dissolved. Stir into butter mixture. Stir in flour mixture until combined. Stir in chocolate and nuts. Cover and refrigerate dough for approximately 2 hours.

2.   Preheat oven to 350°F. Lightly butter two baking sheets or line sheets with baking parchment.

3.   Drop dough by rounded tablespoonfuls (see Note) onto prepared baking sheet, leaving about 2 inches between cookies. Bake one sheet at a time, for 9 to 14 minutes,

or until bottoms of cookies are lightly browned. Remove baking sheet to a wire rack and cool for about 3 minutes. Using a metal spatula, transfer cookies to wire racks and cool completely. Repeat until all dough is used. When cool, store cookies in an airtight container.

These cookies freeze well.

Makes approximately 26 cookies

Note: For crisper cookies, reduce flour to 1¼ cups. For a stronger coffee flavor, use 1 teaspoon instant espresso powder.

To toast almonds, place them in a single layer on a baking sheet and bake at 350°F. for 5 to 7 minutes, shaking sheet a couple of times, until nuts are lightly browned.

For more uniform cookies, chill dough until firm enough to shape. Roll each rounded tablespoonful into a ball and place on prepared baking sheet. Flatten slightly and proceed as above.

Quick Chocolate Brownies and Bars

· AWESOME FUDGY BROWNIES ·

Bittersweet chocolate plus an extra boost of pure chocolate flavor from unsweetened chocolate makes these dense brownies the perfect choice for satisfying an intense chocolate craving. Try using them as the base for a decadent brownie sundae.

1 cup (2 sticks) unsalted butter
9 ounces bittersweet chocolate, broken
  into pieces
4 ounces unsweetened chocolate, broken
  into pieces
4 large eggs, at room temperature
1 cup firmly packed brown sugar

1/2 cup granulated sugar
1 tablespoon vanilla extract
1 cup all-purpose flour
1/4 teaspoon salt
1 1/2 cups chopped walnuts or pecans
  (optional)

1.   Preheat oven to 350°F. Line a 13 × 9-inch baking pan with aluminum foil so that foil extends 2 inches beyond the two long sides of pan. Lightly butter bottom and sides of foil-lined pan.

2.   In a microwave-safe bowl, heat butter and chocolates in a microwave oven on HIGH for 1 to 3 minutes, stirring halfway through cooking, until chocolate is melted (or use a double boiler over hot, not simmering, water). Let stand at room temperature for 20 minutes.

3.   In a large bowl, using a hand-held electric mixer set at medium-high speed, beat eggs and sugars for 2 to 3 minutes, or until light in color. Beat in chocolate mixture and vanilla until blended. Beat in flour and salt. Using a wooden spoon, stir in nuts, if desired.

4.   Scrape batter into prepared pan and spread evenly. Bake for 25 to 30 minutes, or until a cake tester inserted 2 inches from center comes out with fudgy crumbs. Do not overbake.

5.   Remove pan to a wire rack. Cool for about 15 minutes. Using the two ends of foil as handles, lift brownies out of pan and cool on foil for at least 2 hours before cutting into squares. Store completely cooled brownies in an airtight container at cool room temperature.

These brownies freeze well.

Makes 20 brownies

· BLACK FOREST BROWNIES ·

The classic combination of chocolate and cherries creates brownies for the sophisticated palate.

1 cup all-purpose flour
1/2 teaspoon baking powder
1/4 teaspoon salt
1/2 cup (1 stick) unsalted butter, at room temperature
1 cup granulated sugar
2 large eggs, at room temperature

6 ounces bittersweet chocolate, melted and cooled
1 teaspoon vanilla extract
2/3 cup coarsely chopped dried tart cherries (see Note)
1/2 cup miniature semisweet chocolate chips

1. Preheat oven to 350°F. Lightly butter a 9-inch-square baking pan. Lightly dust with flour and tap out excess.

2. In a small bowl, stir together flour, baking powder, and salt. In a large bowl, using a hand-held electric mixer, cream together butter and sugar until light and fluffy. One at a time, add eggs, beating well after each addition. Beat in chocolate and vanilla. Stir in flour mixture until blended. Stir in cherries and chips.

3. Scrape batter into prepared pan and spread evenly. Bake for 30 to 40 minutes, or until a cake tester inserted in center comes out with fudgy crumbs. Cool brownies in pan on a wire rack. Cut into squares.

These brownies freeze well.

Makes 16 brownies

Note: Dried cherries are often available at gourmet food stores, or can be ordered by mail (page 12). Chopped pitted prunes can be substituted for dried cherries.

To store leftover dried cherries, place cherries in original wrapper in a plastic bag or airtight container. Refrigerate for 4 to 6 months. Freeze for longer storage.

• BOURBON PECAN BROWNIES •

Indulge yourself with these pecan brownies spiked with bourbon.

9 ounces bittersweet chocolate, broken
    into pieces
6 ounces unsweetened chocolate, broken
    into pieces
3/4 cup (1 1/2 sticks) unsalted butter, at
    room temperature
1 1/2 cups firmly packed brown sugar

3 large eggs, at room temperature
1/3 cup bourbon
1 teaspoon vanilla extract
1 1/4 cups all-purpose flour
1/4 teaspoon salt
1 1/2 cups chopped pecans

1. Preheat oven to 350°F. Line a 13 × 9-inch baking pan with aluminum foil so that foil extends 2 inches beyond the two long sides of the pan. Lightly butter bottom and sides of foil-lined pan.

2. In a microwave-safe bowl, heat chocolates and butter in a microwave oven on HIGH for 1 to 3 minutes, stirring halfway through cooking, until chocolate is melted (or use a double boiler over hot, not simmering, water). Let stand at room temperature for 10 minutes.

3. In a large bowl, using a hand-held electric mixer set at medium-high speed, beat together sugar and eggs for 1 to 2 minutes, or until light in color. Beat in chocolate mixture, bourbon, and vanilla. Beat in flour and salt until just combined. Using a wooden spoon, stir in nuts.

4. Scrape batter into prepared pan and spread evenly. Bake for 25 to 30 minutes, or until a cake tester inserted in center comes out with fudgy crumbs. Do not overbake.

5. Remove pan to a wire rack. Cool for about 15 minutes. Using the two ends of the foil as handles, lift brownies out of pan and cool on foil for at least 2 hours before cutting into squares. Store completely cooled brownies in an airtight container at cool room temperature.

These brownies freeze well.

Makes 20 brownies

· CHOCOLATE CHIP CHERRY BLONDIES ·

The tart flavor of dried cherries complements the chocolate in these chewy bars. Also try the Apricot White Chocolate Blondies variation on the next page.

1 cup all-purpose flour
1 teaspoon baking powder
¼ teaspoon salt
¼ cup unsalted butter, at room temperature
½ cup firmly packed light brown sugar
1 large egg, at room temperature

1 teaspoon vanilla extract
½ cup semisweet chocolate chips
¼ cup milk chocolate chips
½ cup coarsely chopped dried tart cherries (see Note)
⅓ cup coarsely chopped, toasted slivered almonds (see Note)

1. Preheat oven to 350°F. Butter an 8-inch-square baking pan. Lightly dust with flour and tap out excess.

2. In a small bowl, stir together flour, baking powder, and salt. In a large bowl, using a wooden spoon, cream together butter and sugar until combined. Stir in egg and vanilla until blended. Stir in flour mixture just until combined. Stir in chips, cherries, and nuts.

3. Scrape batter into a prepared baking pan and spread evenly. Bake for 25 to 30 minutes, or until a cake tester inserted in center comes out with fudgy crumbs.

4. Cool pan on a wire rack. Cut blondies into 16 squares. Store cooled blondies in an airtight container at room temperature.

Makes 16 blondies

Variation: For Apricot White Chocolate Blondies, substitute 3 ounces white chocolate, chopped, for the 1/2 cup semisweet chocolate chips and 1/4 cup milk chocolate chips; 1/2 cup chopped dried apricots for the dried tart cherries; and 1/3 cup coarsely chopped pecans or walnuts for the almonds.

Note: Dried cherries are often available in gourmet food stores, or can be ordered by mail (page 12). If desired, reserve 2 tablespoons of semisweet chocolate chips and sprinkle them over blondies before baking.

To toast almonds, place them in a single layer on a baking sheet and bake at 350°F. for 5 to 7 minutes, shaking sheet a couple of times, until nuts are lightly browned.

· CHOCOLATE CHUNK BLONDIES ·

Here's an easy, sturdy treat that's great for packing in lunchboxes.

2 cups all-purpose flour
2 teaspoons baking powder
¹/₂ teaspoon salt
¹/₂ cup (1 stick) unsalted butter, at room
*   temperature*
1 cup firmly packed light brown sugar

¹/₂ cup granulated sugar
2 large eggs, at room temperature
1 tablespoon vanilla extract
12 ounces bittersweet, milk, and/or white
*   chocolate, cut into ¹/₂-inch pieces*
1 cup coarsely broken walnuts or pecans

1. Preheat oven to 350°F. Line a 13 × 9-inch baking pan with aluminum foil so that foil extends 2 inches beyond the two long sides of the pan. Lightly butter bottom and sides of foil-lined pan.

2. In a large bowl, stir together flour, baking powder, and salt. In another large bowl, using a hand-held electric mixer set at medium speed, beat butter and sugars together for 1 to 2 minutes, until combined. One at a time, add eggs, beating well after each addition. Beat in vanilla. On low speed, add flour mixture and beat just until combined. Using a wooden spoon, stir in chocolate and nuts.

3. Scrape batter into prepared pan and spread evenly. Bake for 30 to 35 minutes, or until blondies are set. Do not overbake.

4. Remove pan to a wire rack. Cool for about 30 minutes. Using the two ends of the foil as handles, lift blondie "rectangle" out of pan and cool on foil for at least 2 hours

before cutting into squares. Store completely cooled blondies in an airtight container at cool room temperature.

These blondies freeze well.

Makes 20 blondies

• CHOCOLATE ORANGE BROWNIES •

Orange and chocolate are a match made in heaven. Place a doily or stencil over the top of these fudgy brownies, sprinkle with confectioners' sugar, and remove the doily or stencil to create an elegant look. Garnish each dessert plate with a twist of orange and a couple of raspberries to complete the look.

³/₄ cup (1¹/₂ sticks) unsalted butter
8 ounces semisweet chocolate, broken into
  pieces
4 ounces unsweetened chocolate, broken
  into pieces
1 cup granulated sugar
¹/₂ cup firmly packed brown sugar

3 large eggs, at room temperature
¹/₃ cup orange-flavored liqueur, such as
  Cointreau
1 teaspoon vanilla extract
³/₄ teaspoon grated orange peel
1¹/₄ cups all-purpose flour
¹/₄ teaspoon salt

1.   Preheat oven to 350°F. Line a 13 × 9-inch baking pan with aluminum foil so that foil extends 2 inches beyond the two long sides of the pan. Lightly butter bottom and sides of foil-lined pan.

2.   In a microwave-safe bowl, heat butter and chocolates in a microwave oven on HIGH for 1 to 3 minutes, stirring halfway through cooking, until chocolate is melted (or use a double boiler over hot, not simmering, water). Let stand at room temperature for 10 minutes.

3.   In a large bowl, using a hand-held electric mixer set at medium-high speed, beat together sugars and eggs for 1 to 2 minutes, or until light in color. Beat in

chocolate mixture, liqueur, vanilla, and orange peel. Beat in flour and salt until just combined.

4.   Scrape batter into prepared pan and spread evenly. Bake for 25 to 30 minutes, or until a cake tester inserted in center comes out with fudgy crumbs. Do not overbake.

5.   Remove pan to a wire rack. Cool for about 15 minutes. Using the two ends of the foil as handles, lift brownie "rectangle" out of pan and cool on foil for at least 2 hours before cutting into squares. Store completely cooled brownies in an airtight container at cool room temperature.

These brownies freeze well.

Makes 20 brownies

• DEEP-DISH BROWNIE PIZZA •

Here's a brownie that's done in the round! Chunks of chocolate decorate the top of this sweet "pie." Serve wedges with a scoop of ice cream and drizzle with Chocolate Sauce (page 132) for a fun and decadent dessert.

½ cup (1 stick) unsalted butter
2 ounces unsweetened chocolate
2 large eggs, at room temperature
½ cup granulated sugar
1½ teaspoons vanilla extract
½ cup all-purpose flour
⅛ teaspoon salt
½ cup coarsely broken walnuts or pecans

3 ounces bittersweet chocolate, cut into ½-inch pieces, divided
3 ounces milk chocolate, cut into ½-inch pieces, divided
3 ounces white chocolate, cut into ½-inch pieces, divided

1. Preheat oven to 350°F. Lightly butter a 9-inch pie plate.
2. In a microwave-safe bowl, heat butter and chocolate in a microwave oven on HIGH for 1 to 3 minutes, stirring halfway through cooking, until chocolate is melted (or use a double boiler over hot, not simmering, water). Let stand at room temperature for 20 minutes.
3. In a large bowl, using a hand-held electric mixer set at medium-high speed, beat eggs and sugar for 2 to 3 minutes, or until light in color. Beat in chocolate mixture and vanilla until blended. Beat in flour and salt. Using a wooden spoon, stir in nuts along with half the bittersweet, milk, and white chocolate pieces.

4. Scrape batter into prepared pie plate and spread evenly. Sprinkle surface with remaining chocolate pieces. Bake for 25 to 30 minutes, or until a cake tester inserted 2 inches from center comes out with fudgy crumbs. Do not overbake.

5. Remove pan to a wire rack to cool. Cut into wedges to serve. Store completely cooled "pizza" in an airtight container at cool room temperature.

This brownie pizza freezes well.

Makes 8 to 10 servings

· PEANUT BUTTER BROWNIES ·

These extra-fudgy brownies are filled with chopped peanut butter cups.

4 ounces bittersweet chocolate, chopped
⅓ cup (5⅓ tablespoons) unsalted butter
¾ cup all-purpose flour
⅛ teaspoon salt

¾ cup granulated sugar
2 large eggs, at room temperature
1 teaspoon vanilla extract
7 chocolate-covered peanut butter cups
(.6 ounce each) or 5 (.8 ounce) cups,
coarsely chopped

1. Preheat oven to 350°F. Butter an 8-inch-square baking pan. Lightly dust with flour and tap out excess.

2. In a small heavy saucepan, over low heat, stir chocolate and butter, until melted. Cool for 10 minutes. In a small bowl, stir together flour and salt. In a large bowl, with a fork, beat together sugar and eggs. Beat in chocolate mixture and vanilla. Stir in flour mixture until blended.

3. Scrape half the batter into prepared pan and spread evenly. Sprinkle with chopped candy. Scrape remaining batter into pan and spread evenly to cover candy. Bake for 25 to 35 minutes, or until a cake tester inserted in center comes out with fudgy crumbs. Cool brownies in pan on a wire rack. Cut into squares.

Makes 16 brownies

Variation: Substitute 2 (2.07 ounces) Snickers bars for the peanut butter cups.

• TURTLE BARS •

A cross between a cookie and candy, these caramel pecan bars are inspired by the classic candy.

COOKIE CRUST
1 cup all-purpose flour
1/4 cup finely chopped pecans
1/2 teaspoon baking powder
1/4 teaspoon salt
*1/3 cup (5 1/3 tablespoons) unsalted
  butter, at room temperature*

*2/3 cup firmly packed light brown
  sugar*
1 large egg, at room temperature
1/2 teaspoon vanilla extract

TOPPING
16 caramel candies
1 1/2 tablespoons milk

1/2 cup chopped pecans
1 1/4 cups semisweet chocolate chips

1. *To prepare cookie crust:* Lightly butter a 9-inch-square baking pan.
2. In a medium bowl, stir together flour, pecans, baking powder, and salt. In a large bowl, using a wooden spoon, cream together butter and sugar until combined. Stir in egg and vanilla until blended. Stir in flour mixture until combined. Cover and refrigerate for 1 hour.
3. Preheat oven to 375°F.
4. Pat dough into prepared baking pan. Bake for 15 to 20 minutes, or until lightly

browned. Remove pan to a wire rack and cool for 30 minutes. With a small metal spatula, loosen edges.

5. *To prepare topping:* In a small heavy saucepan, over low heat, melt caramels with milk, stirring, until smooth. Pour over cooled crust and spread to cover. Sprinkle caramel with nuts. Press down lightly. Cover and refrigerate for about 30 minutes.

6. Preheat oven to 375°F.

7. Sprinkle caramel and nuts with chips. Bake for 3 minutes, or until chips are melted. Spread to a smooth layer. Refrigerate for 2 hours or until firm. Let pan sit at room temperature for 30 minutes. Remove baked square from pan. Using a sharp serrated knife and a sawing motion, cut into bars.

Makes 32 bars

· WALNUT LOVERS' BROWNIES ·

If you love walnuts, then these brownies are for you. Rich fudgy brownies are studded with walnuts and sport a crunchy walnut layer on top.

BROWNIE LAYER

1/2 cup (1 stick) unsalted butter
4 ounces semisweet chocolate
2 ounces unsweetened chocolate
2 large eggs, at room temperature
2/3 cup firmly packed brown sugar

1/4 cup granulated sugar
1 teaspoon vanilla extract
1/2 cup all-purpose flour
1/4 teaspoon salt
1/2 cup chopped walnuts

WALNUT TOPPING

1/3 cup firmly packed brown sugar
2 tablespoons unsalted butter
1 large egg, at room temperature

1 tablespoon all-purpose flour
1 teaspoon vanilla extract
2 cups chopped walnuts

1.   Preheat oven to 350°F. Line a 9-inch-square baking pan with aluminum foil so that foil extends 2 inches beyond two opposite sides of pan. Lightly butter bottom and sides of foil-lined pan.

2.   *To prepare brownies:* In a microwave-safe bowl, heat butter and chocolates in a microwave oven on HIGH for 1 to 3 minutes, stirring halfway through cooking, until chocolate is melted (or use a double boiler over hot, not simmering, water). Let stand at room temperature for 10 minutes.

3. In a large bowl, using a hand-held electric mixer set at medium-high speed, beat eggs and sugars for about 3 minutes, or until light in color. Beat in chocolate mixture and vanilla until blended. Mix in flour and salt until just combined. Stir in walnuts. Scrape batter into prepared baking pan and spread evenly.

4. *To prepare topping:* In a large microwave-safe bowl, heat brown sugar and butter in a microwave oven on HIGH for 30 to 60 seconds, or just until butter is melted. Stir in egg, flour, and vanilla until combined. Stir in walnuts until combined. Spread mixture evenly over brownie batter.

5. Bake for 35 to 40 minutes, or until a cake tester inserted in center comes out with fudgy crumbs. Do not overbake.

6. Remove pan to a wire rack. Cool for about 5 minutes. Using the two ends of the foil as handles, lift the brownie "square" out of pan and cool on foil for at least 2 hours before cutting into squares. Store completely cooled brownies in an airtight container at cool room temperature.

Makes 16 brownies

Quick Chocolate Ice Creams and Puddings

· CHOCOLATE BREAD PUDDING ·

This old-fashioned dessert is delicious served warm, topped with whipped cream or vanilla ice cream.

6 slices firm-crumb white bread
2 tablespoons unsalted butter, at room
  temperature
⅓ cup miniature semisweet chocolate
  chips
⅓ cup raisins
⅓ cup chopped toasted pecans or walnuts
  (see Note)

2 cups milk
6 ounces bittersweet chocolate, chopped
½ cup firmly packed light brown sugar
4 large eggs, at room temperature
1 teaspoon vanilla extract

1.   Preheat oven to 350°F. Lightly butter a 9-inch-square baking dish.
2.   Spread bread lightly with butter. Cut each slice into 4 triangles. Place in prepared baking dish. Sprinkle with chips, raisins, and nuts.
3.   In a 2-quart saucepan, heat milk until small bubbles form around edge of pan. Remove from heat. Immediately add bittersweet chocolate and stir until melted. Stir in sugar until dissolved. In a small bowl with a fork, lightly beat eggs. Stir in approximately ½ cup hot milk mixture until blended. Pour egg mixture back into saucepan. Stir in vanilla. Pour over bread. Press down bread to soak with egg mixture. Place baking dish in a larger baking pan. Carefully pour enough hot water into larger pan to go 1 inch up sides of smaller pan. Bake for 50 to 60 minutes, or until a knife inserted in center comes

out clean. Carefully remove baking dish. Cover pudding and store in refrigerator for up to 4 days.

Makes 6 to 8 servings

Variation: For Raspberry Bread Pudding, spread 3 slices white bread with 1 tablespoon softened cream cheese each. Spread the remaining 3 slices of white bread with 1 teaspoon of seedless raspberry jam each. Put slices together to form 3 cream cheese and jam sandwiches. Cut each sandwich into 4 triangles. Proceed as above, omitting butter and raisins. Substitute toasted slivered almonds for pecans.

Note: To reheat pudding, place one serving in a microwave-safe container and microwave on MEDIUM (50 percent) for 30 to 60 seconds (depending on amount of pudding) until heated through.

To toast nuts, place them in a single layer on a baking sheet and bake at 350°F. for 5 to 7 minutes, shaking sheet a couple of times, until nuts are lightly browned.

· CHOCOLATE TIRAMISÙ ·

This version of the popular Italian dessert is made with chocolate cake instead of the traditional lady fingers. We've even included a super-quick variation.

*1 pound mascarpone (see Note) or cream
    cheese, at room temperature*
7 large egg yolks
⅔ cup granulated sugar
⅛ teaspoon salt
⅔ cup milk
2 teaspoons vanilla extract
*1⅔ cups espresso or strongly brewed
    coffee*

¼ cup coffee-flavored liqueur
*3 ounces bittersweet chocolate, grated or
    ground (see Note)*
*1½ (14- to 16-ounce) loaves chocolate or
    chocolate marble pound cake (see
    Note), cut into ⅜- to ½-inch-thick slices*
2 to 3 teaspoons unsweetened cocoa powder

1. In a medium bowl with a fork, beat cheese until soft. Set aside.

2. Place a large metal bowl (approximately 4-quart) over a pot of boiling water. (The bottom of bowl should touch water.) Using a hand-held electric mixer set on medium speed, beat yolks, sugar, and salt for 1 minute. With mixer on low speed, gradually beat in milk. Increase speed to medium, cooking and stirring constantly, until mixture thickens and temperature of mixture reaches 160°F., about 5 minutes (see Note).

3. Remove bowl from heat. Beat mixture for 1 minute. Beat in cheese and vanilla until blended. Set custard aside.

4. Stir together espresso and liqueur. Place half the espresso mixture into a small

shallow bowl. Quickly dip each cake slice into espresso. Do not soak. Place cake slices, moist sides up, in bottom of a 13 × 9-inch baking dish to make a single layer. (Do not use a metal pan.) If necessary, trim slices to fit, covering bottom of dish. Pour slightly less than half the custard mixture over cake and spread to cover. Sprinkle with grated chocolate.

5. Repeat procedure with remaining cake and espresso mixture. Top with remaining custard mixture and carefully spread to cover.

6. Sift cocoa over top of tiramisù to coat evenly. Cover and refrigerate 8 hours, or overnight.

Makes 12 servings

Note: Mascarpone cheese is similar to cream cheese and is found in Italian markets and many supermarkets.

To prepare finely ground chocolate: Process coarsely chopped chocolate in container of a food processor fitted with a steel blade until ground.

Fat-free or low-fat chocolate or marble pound cake can be used in this recipe.

A deep 4- or 5-quart metal bowl works best for this recipe to prevent custard from splattering when beating. After 5 minutes, stop beating with electric mixer and stir with a wooden spoon, while checking the temperature of custard.

For a Super-Quick Tiramisù: If you're in a hurry, instead of layering cake with custard, try using this whipped cream to spread over cake. Omit egg yolks, granulated sugar, and milk. Instead, using a hand-held electric mixer with chilled beaters and a chilled bowl, beat 2 cups chilled heavy (whipping) cream, 1 cup confectioners' sugar, salt, and vanilla until stiff peaks form. Beat in mascarpone or cream cheese. Proceed as directed.

· COFFEE TOFFEE ICE CREAM ·

This simplified version of coffee ice cream uses instant coffee to save time. Be sure the milk and cream are well chilled before starting.

2 tablespoons instant coffee powder
1 cup whole milk, well chilled
⅔ cup granulated sugar (see Note)
Dash salt
2 cups heavy (whipping) cream, well chilled

2 teaspoons vanilla extract
3 bars (1.4 ounces each) milk chocolate–coated toffee, chopped

1.   In a large bowl, gradually stir milk into instant coffee until dissolved. Stir in sugar and salt, until dissolved. Stir in cream and vanilla. Pour into container of an ice cream maker.

2.   Freeze according to manufacturer's directions. Add candy and process for 15 seconds, or until evenly distributed.

3.   Quickly remove ice cream from ice cream maker. Cover and freeze for 8 hours, or until firm.

Makes approximately 1 quart

Note: For a variation, use ⅓ cup firmly packed light brown sugar and ⅓ cup granulated sugar instead of ⅔ cup granulated sugar.

· COOKIES AND ICE CREAM BOMBE ·

Prepare this super-quick ice cream bombe ahead of time and serve with Chocolate Sauce (page 132) or Raspberry Sauce (page 99) (or use commercially prepared sauces or syrups) for a dessert that's perfect for entertaining.

We've selected vanilla, banana, and chocolate ice cream, but you can make up your own ice cream (or frozen yogurt) and cookie combinations. Crushed candy can also be substituted for up to 1 cup of the cookies.

2 cups vanilla or chocolate chip ice cream
14 cream-filled chocolate sandwich cookies (about 5 ounces), broken into small pieces, divided (makes about 2 cups) (see Note)

2 cups banana ice cream (or coffee, peanut butter, butter pecan, or your favorite flavor)
2½ cups chocolate ice cream
Chocolate Sauce or commercially prepared fudge sauce

1. Lightly oil a 1½-quart ice cream mold or metal bowl. Place in freezer for 30 minutes. Soften ice cream at room temperature for approximately 10 minutes.

2. Place vanilla ice cream in bottom of chilled mold or bowl and spread evenly. Sprinkle with approximately ½ cup cookie pieces (see Note).

3. Top with banana ice cream and spread evenly. Sprinkle with approximately ¾ cup cookie pieces.

4. Top with chocolate ice cream and spread evenly. Sprinkle with remaining cookie pieces. Cover and freeze for at least 8 hours, or until firm.

5. To serve, loosen edge with a metal spatula. Invert onto a serving platter and cover with a damp warm dish towel for 15 seconds. Remove mold. Slice bombe into wedges and serve with Chocolate Sauce.

Makes 6 to 8 servings

Note: When substituting cookies, use an equal weight such as approximately 5 ounces of chocolate chip cookies, peanut butter cream sandwich cookies, or homemade cookies for the cream-filled chocolate sandwich cookies.

If you have difficulty assembling the bombe, place bombe in freezer for 4 to 5 minutes before adding each layer of ice cream.

· INTENSELY CHOCOLATE PUDDING ·

Here's a thick pudding that is very, very chocolaty. Serve it in a stemmed crystal glass, perhaps topped with rosy raspberries and a sprig of mint for an elegant finale. Instant espresso powder adds extra intenseness to the pudding's chocolate flavor.

1 cup granulated sugar
¹/₃ cup cornstarch
Dash salt
4 large egg yolks, lightly beaten
3¹/₂ cups whole milk
6 ounces bittersweet chocolate, finely chopped

2 ounces unsweetened chocolate, finely chopped
2 teaspoons vanilla extract
¹/₂ teaspoon instant espresso powder (optional)

1. In a large heavy saucepan, stir together sugar, cornstarch, and salt. Gradually whisk in egg yolks until combined. Gradually whisk in milk.

2. Cook mixture over medium-high heat, stirring constantly with a whisk for about 15 to 20 minutes, or until mixture thickens. Remove pan from heat and whisk in chocolates, vanilla, and espresso powder, if desired, whisking until smooth. Quickly pour mixture through a strainer into a bowl. Cover surface of pudding with a piece of plastic wrap to prevent a skin from forming. Refrigerate until ready to use.

Makes 8 servings or enough to fill one 9-inch pie

• MOCHA ICE CREAM •

Try this rich mocha ice cream topped with Chocolate Sauce (page 132), Chocolate Marshmallow Topping (page 131), or Raspberry Sauce (page 99).

1 cup whole milk
5 ounces bittersweet chocolate, chopped
2 tablespoons instant coffee powder
²/₃ cup granulated sugar

Dash salt
2 cups heavy (whipping) cream, well chilled
2 teaspoons vanilla extract

1. In a small saucepan, heat milk until small bubbles form around edge of pan. Stir in chocolate and instant coffee powder until blended. Continue to cook over medium-low heat, stirring constantly, until all chocolate is dissolved. Pour into a large bowl, stir in sugar and salt until dissolved. Let sit at room temperature for 10 minutes. Cover and refrigerate for 1 to 2 hours, or until cold, stirring occasionally.
2. Stir in cream and vanilla until blended. Pour into container of an ice cream maker.
3. Freeze according to manufacturer's directions. Quickly remove ice cream from ice cream maker. Cover and freeze for 8 hours, or until firm.

Makes approximately 1 quart

• PEANUT BUTTER CANDY–CHUNK ICE CREAM •

Be creative with this peanut butter–based ice cream by adding chunks of your favorite candy bar. We suggest adding 1 cup of chopped candy, but you can add more or less to suit your taste.

1/2 cup creamy peanut butter
1 cup whole milk, well chilled
3/4 cup firmly packed light brown sugar
2 cups heavy (whipping) cream, well
    chilled

2 teaspoons vanilla extract
1 cup chopped candy, such as milk chocolate,
    Reese's peanut butter cups,
    Butterfingers, milk chocolate–coated
    toffee bars, etc. (approximately 5
    ounces)

1. In a large bowl, gradually whisk milk into peanut butter. Stir in sugar until dissolved. Stir in cream and vanilla. Pour into container of an ice cream maker.

2. Freeze according to manufacturer's directions. Add candy and process for 15 seconds, or until evenly distributed.

3. Quickly remove ice cream from ice cream maker. Cover and freeze for 8 hours, or until firm.

Makes approximately 1 quart

· SPEEDY BROWNIE CHUNK ICE CREAM ·

Here's a great way to recycle leftover brownies. Cut them into ½-inch cubes and stir them into the ice cream. This recipe was extra easy when we tested it in the type of ice cream maker that uses a frozen cylinder, such as a Donvier. To make ice cream at the spur of the moment, store the cylinder in your freezer.

*1½ cups heavy (whipping) cream, well
 chilled
1½ cups whole milk, well chilled*

*½ cup superfine sugar
2 teaspoons vanilla extract
Scant 1 cup of ½-inch brownie cubes*

In a large bowl, whisk together cream, milk, sugar, and vanilla until sugar is dissolved. Pour mixture into frozen cylinder of ice cream maker. Freeze according to manufacturer's directions, adding the brownie chunks halfway through freezing time. Store leftover ice cream in freezer.

Makes approximately 1 quart

Quick Chocolate
Pies, Tarts, and
Pastries

• BROWNIE-BOTTOM ICE CREAM PIE •

Serve this simple, yet delicious ice cream pie with homemade Chocolate Sauce (page 132) or commercially prepared chocolate sauce or syrup. Or try one of the following simple sauces—Strawberry or Raspberry Sauce.

BROWNIE CRUST

$^1/_2$ cup all-purpose flour	3 tablespoons vegetable oil
$^1/_4$ teaspoon baking powder	$^1/_2$ cup firmly packed light brown sugar
$^1/_8$ teaspoon salt	1 large egg, at room temperature
3 ounces bittersweet chocolate, coarsely chopped	1 teaspoon vanilla extract
2 tablespoons water	

ICE CREAM FILLING

1 quart ice cream, such as mocha chip, chocolate chip, coffee, vanilla fudge, or your favorite flavor (see Note)	Strawberry or Raspberry Sauce (recipe follows) or Chocolate Sauce
$1^1/_2$ ounces bittersweet chocolate, grated or finely ground (see Note)	

   1. *To prepare brownie crust:* Preheat oven to 325°F. Generously butter a 9-inch pie plate. Lightly dust plate with flour and tap out excess.

   2. In a small bowl, stir together flour, baking powder, and salt. In top of a double

boiler over hot, not simmering, water, heat chocolate and water, stirring until smooth. Remove top of double boiler and let cool.

3. In a large bowl, with a fork, cream together oil and sugar until combined. Beat in egg and vanilla. Beat in chocolate mixture. Stir in flour mixture until blended.

4. Scrape batter into prepared pie plate. Bake for 20 to 25 minutes, or until a cake tester inserted in center comes out clean. Completely cool brownie in plate on a wire rack.

5. With a small metal spatula carefully loosen brownie from plate, but do not remove. With a paper towel, clean edges of pie plate of flour and crumbs.

6. *To assemble:* Place brownie in freezer while ice cream is softening at room temperature for approximately 10 to 15 minutes. Mound ice cream on top of brownie crust and smooth surface. Sprinkle with chocolate. Cover loosely with plastic wrap. Freeze 8 hours, or until firm.

Makes approximately 8 servings

Note: If desired, top crust with two flavors of ice cream. Pie can be garnished with 2 tablespoons of miniature semisweet chocolate chips or chopped nuts instead of the grated chocolate.

To prepare finely ground chocolate: Process bittersweet chocolate in container of a food processor fitted with a steel blade until ground.

· STRAWBERRY OR RASPBERRY SAUCE ·

1 package (10 ounces) frozen
strawberries or raspberries in syrup,
thawed

1 teaspoon cornstarch
1 teaspoon cold water
¼ teaspoon vanilla extract

In blender container, process berries with syrup until just puréed. Pour mixture into a 1-quart saucepan. In a small bowl or cup, stir cornstarch and water until dissolved. Add to saucepan. Cook over medium heat, stirring constantly, for 5 minutes, or until mixture comes to a boil and thickens slightly. Remove from heat. Stir in vanilla. Cool for 10 minutes. Refrigerate until chilled.

Makes approximately 1 cup

· CHOCOLATE CANDY CREAM PIE ·

This is a great way to use up leftover Halloween candy, but you can make it at any time of year.

*1 6-ounce commercially prepared
graham cracker pie shell (see Note)*

FILLING

*⅓ cup commercially prepared chocolate
fudge sauce, at room temperature
(see Note)*
*1 cup heavy (whipping) cream, well
chilled*

3 tablespoons confectioners' sugar
½ teaspoon vanilla extract
*½ cup chopped candy bar pieces (such as
Butterfingers, Reese's peanut butter
cups, etc.)*

TOPPING

*1 cup heavy (whipping) cream, well
chilled*
*⅔ cup commercially prepared chocolate
fudge sauce, at room temperature
(see Note)*

*1 to 2 tablespoons grated bittersweet
chocolate, chocolate sprinkles, or
miniature semisweet chocolate chips*

1. *To prepare filling:* Spread pie shell with chocolate fudge sauce.
2. In a chilled bowl, using a hand-held electric mixer with chilled beaters, beat

cream, sugar, and vanilla until thick and fluffy. Fold in candy. Scrape into pie shell and spread evenly.

3. *To prepare topping:* In same bowl, using a hand-held electric mixer with same beaters, beat cream and chocolate fudge sauce until thick and fluffy. Scrape into pie shell. Mound mixture and smooth surface. Sprinkle with grated chocolate and freeze for 6 hours, or until firm. Let sit at room temperature for 10 minutes before serving.

Makes 6 to 8 servings

Note: You can substitute a homemade 8-inch graham cracker pie shell.

If necessary, soften chocolate fudge sauce according to container directions and cool.

· CHOCOLATE CHERRY PIE ·

Keep dried tart cherries on hand and you can enjoy this tempting cherry pie all year round. Dried cherries are often available at gourmet food stores, or can be ordered by mail (page 12).

PIE CRUST

1¼ cups all-purpose flour
1 tablespoon firmly packed light brown sugar
¼ teaspoon salt

3 tablespoons unsalted butter, chilled
3 tablespoons solid vegetable shortening
2 to 3 tablespoons ice water

FILLING

3 large eggs, at room temperature
⅔ cup firmly packed light brown sugar
⅔ cup light corn syrup
1 tablespoon unsalted butter, melted and cooled
3 tablespoons all-purpose flour

⅛ teaspoon salt
1¼ cups coarsely chopped dried tart cherries
¾ cup semisweet chocolate chips

1.   *To prepare pie crust:* In a large bowl, stir together flour, sugar, and salt. Cut butter into ½-inch cubes and distribute them over flour mixture. Add vegetable shortening. With a pastry blender or two knives used scissors fashion, cut in butter and shortening

until mixture resembles coarse crumbs. Stir in 2 tablespoons of ice water. If necessary, add enough of remaining water to form a soft dough.

2. Preheat oven to 350°F.

3. Flatten ball and place on a lightly floured 15-inch piece of wax paper. Roll out dough to an 11-inch circle (approximately ⅛ inch thickness). Invert dough over a 9-inch pie pan. Remove wax paper. Line pan with dough and pinch edges. Place pie shell in freezer for 10 minutes while preparing filling.

4. *To prepare filling:* In a medium bowl, stir together eggs and sugar until blended. Stir in corn syrup and butter. Stir in flour and salt until combined. Stir in cherries and chips. Scrape mixture into pie crust and spread evenly. Bake pie for 45 to 60 minutes, or until a cake tester inserted 1 inch from center comes out clean (excluding melted chocolate). If necessary, to prevent overbrowning, carefully cover edges of pie crust with foil during last 10 minutes of baking. Transfer to a wire rack to cool. Store cooled pie in an airtight container in refrigerator. Serve at room temperature.

Makes 6 to 8 servings

Note: You can substitute a frozen 9-inch deep-dish pie shell for homemade pie crust. Do not thaw before using.

• CHOCOLATE CHIP PECAN PIE •

The decadence of pecan pie is stepped up a notch with the addition of chocolate chips. It's delicious served warm with a scoop of vanilla ice cream.

*Pie Crust (page 102) or your favorite
  crust for a 9-inch pie*
3 large eggs, at room temperature
1 cup light corn syrup
¾ cup firmly packed dark brown sugar

1 tablespoon unsalted butter, melted
1 teaspoon vanilla extract
Dash salt
1 cup pecan halves
1 cup semisweet chocolate chips

1. Preheat oven to 350°F.
2. Fit pastry into a 9-inch pie pan.
3. In a large bowl, whisk eggs until frothy. Whisk in corn syrup, sugar, butter, vanilla, and salt. Stir in nuts and chips. Scrape mixture into pie crust and spread evenly. Bake for about 1 hour, or until a cake tester inserted 1 inch from center comes out clean (excluding melted chocolate). If necessary, to prevent overbrowning, carefully cover edge of pie crust with foil during last 10 minutes of baking. Transfer to a wire rack to cool. Store cooled pie in an airtight container in refrigerator. Serve at room temperature.

Makes 6 to 8 servings

Note: This pie has a wet filling. For a firmer filling, stir 1 to 2 tablespoons of all-purpose flour into the filling mixture.

· CHOCOLATE HAZELNUT CREAM PUFFS ·

These delectable pastries are easy to prepare, yet fancy enough to serve at a dinner party. Garnish with shredded chocolate or chocolate-covered coffee bean candies.

1 package (10 ounces) frozen puff pastry shells

³/₄ cup heavy (whipping) cream, well chilled

¹/₃ cup hazelnut chocolate spread (such as Nutella)

1. Bake pastry shells according to package directions. Remove baking sheet to a wire rack to cool for about 3 minutes. Using a metal spatula, transfer pastry shells to a wire rack and cool completely.

2. Immediately before serving, in a small chilled bowl, using a hand-held electric mixer with chilled beaters, beat cream and hazelnut spread until stiff peaks form. Spoon 2 heaping tablespoonfuls of cream mixture into cooled shells or use a pastry bag fitted with a ¹/₂-inch star tip and pipe cream mixture into cooled shells. These pastries are best served soon after preparation.

Makes 6 pastries

· CHOCOLATE PHYLLO ROLL EXTRAVAGANZA ·

Choose from a selection of three delicious fillings for these flaky phyllo rolls. Better yet, make all three or create your own.

CHOCOLATE CHIP ORANGE CHEESE FILLING

1 package (8 ounces) cream cheese, at room temperature
1 large egg yolk, at room temperature
¼ cup confectioners' sugar

1 tablespoon all-purpose flour
¼ teaspoon grated orange peel
¾ cup miniature semisweet chocolate chips

PASTRY

6 to 7 frozen phyllo leaves, thawed
¼ cup (4 tablespoons) unsalted butter, melted

1. *To prepare Chocolate Chip Orange Cheese Filling:* In a small bowl, stir together cream cheese, egg yolk, sugar, flour, and orange peel until blended. Stir in chips.

2. Preheat oven to 350°F.

3. Cut phyllo leaves crosswise into 2 equal-size pieces, each measuring 12 × 8 inches. Cover phyllo with wax paper and then a damp dish towel.

4. Working with two pieces of phyllo at a time, using a pastry brush, lightly coat entire surface of both pieces of phyllo with butter. Place a rounded tablespoonful of filling 1 inch from short edge of each piece of phyllo. Loosely fold long sides in over

mixture. Carefully roll up phyllo, jelly-roll fashion. (If phyllo is torn, some filling may leak out when baked.) Brush roll lightly with butter. Place on an ungreased baking sheet, seam-side down, leaving about 2 inches between rolls. Repeat procedure with remaining ingredients. Bake for 15 to 20 minutes, or until lightly brown. These pastries are best eaten soon after baking.

Makes approximately 12 to 14 rolls

Note: Phyllo dough is wafer-thin pastry available in the frozen food department of many supermarkets. Thaw according to package directions. Although this recipe calls for 6 to 7 leaves of phyllo dough, you may need more because some may be stuck together or torn. (Each package contains approximately 30 leaves.)

For Chocolate Caramel Filling: Stir together 1 large egg (at room temperature), 1 tablespoon light corn syrup, 1 tablespoon confectioners' sugar, and 1 tablespoon all-purpose flour until blended. Stir in 16 diced or coarsely chopped caramel candies and $3/4$ cup miniature semisweet chocolate chips. Proceed as directed.

For Chocolate Coconut Filling: Stir together $3/4$ cup shredded sweetened coconut, $1/2$ cup miniature semisweet chocolate chips, $1/3$ cup chopped walnuts, and $1/2$ cup sweetened condensed milk. Proceed as directed.

· CHOCOLATE PUFFS ·

Frozen puff pastry is the basis for these elegant chocolate pastries. They're great for breakfast served with hot café au lait.

1 sheet frozen puff pastry, thawed
according to package directions
1 bar (3 ounces) dark Swiss chocolate
(such as Lindt), cut into 12 1-inch
squares (see Note)

1 large egg
1 teaspoon water
1 tablespoon finely chopped blanched
almonds
1½ teaspoons granulated sugar

1. Preheat oven to 350°F.
2. Cut pastry into 3 strips along fold lines. Cut each strip into 4 equal pieces (making approximately 2½-inch squares). Place 6 squares on an ungreased baking sheet, leaving about 2 inches between pastries. Stack 2 chocolate squares in center of each pastry square. Top each with a second pastry square. Press edges together with tines of a fork.
3. In a small bowl, stir together egg and water until blended. Brush top of each pastry square with egg mixture. (Do not brush egg mixture on cut edges of pastry.) Sprinkle each with approximately ½ teaspoon chopped nuts and ¼ teaspoon sugar. Bake for approximately 20 minutes, or until puffed and lightly browned. Remove baking sheet to a wire rack to cool for about 3 minutes. Using a metal spatula, transfer pastries to wire rack and cool for approximately 10 minutes. These are best served soon after baking while chocolate is still slightly warm.

Makes 6 pastries

Note: You will need to put together chocolate pieces to form some of the squares. There will be extra chocolate. Or use 1 × 1 × ½-inch chunks of bittersweet chocolate.

· IRRESISTIBLE CHOCOLATE PEANUT BUTTER PIE ·

A rich layer of chocolate ganache (chocolate and cream) forms the base of this pie, which is topped with a fluffy peanut butter and cream cheese mixture. Serve it as a memorable finale at your next get-together.

1 6-ounce commercially prepared
graham cracker or chocolate cookie
crumb pie shell (see Note)

CHOCOLATE LAYER
1 cup heavy (whipping) cream
9 ounces bittersweet chocolate, finely
chopped

PEANUT BUTTER LAYER
8 ounces cream cheese, at room
temperature
1 cup smooth peanut butter
½ teaspoon vanilla extract
1 cup confectioners' sugar

1 cup heavy (whipping) cream, well chilled
2 tablespoons chopped peanuts, for garnish
(optional)

1. *To prepare chocolate layer:* In a medium saucepan over medium-low heat, slowly bring cream to a gentle boil. Remove pan from heat and add chocolate. Let mixture

stand for 1 to 2 minutes and whisk until smooth. Pour chocolate mixture into crust and spread evenly. Refrigerate or freeze for 30 to 60 minutes, or until set.

2. *To prepare peanut butter layer:* In a large bowl, using a hand-held electric mixer set at medium-high speed, cream together cream cheese, peanut butter, and vanilla until blended. Gradually beat in confectioners' sugar just until combined. In a chilled bowl, using a hand-held electric mixer with chilled beaters, beat cream just until stiff peaks begin to form. Using a rubber spatula, stir about one-third of whipped cream into peanut butter mixture until smooth. Gently fold in remaining whipped cream until incorporated. Scrape into pie shell and spread evenly. If desired, sprinkle surface with chopped peanuts. Refrigerate pie for at least 2 hours, or until peanut butter filling is firm.

Makes 6 to 8 servings

Note: You can substitute a homemade 8-inch graham cracker pie shell for the commercially prepared one.

• MOCHA HAZELNUT CREAM PIE •

Coffee, chocolate, and hazelnut combine to create a tempting grown-up dessert—that's as easy as pie.

1 6-ounce commercially prepared
graham cracker pie shell (see Note)

FILLING

⅓ cup commercially prepared chocolate
fudge sauce, at room temperature
(see Note)
1 cup heavy (whipping) cream, well
chilled
2 teaspoons instant coffee powder

¼ cup confectioners' sugar
½ teaspoon vanilla extract
½ cup chopped milk chocolate–coated toffee
bars or other chopped candy bars

TOPPING

1 cup heavy (whipping) cream, well
chilled
⅓ cup hazelnut chocolate spread (such
as Nutella), at room temperature

1 to 2 tablespoons grated bittersweet
chocolate, chocolate sprinkles, or
miniature semisweet chocolate chips

1. *To prepare filling:* Spread pie shell with chocolate fudge sauce. Stir cream with instant coffee powder until dissolved.

2. In a chilled bowl, using a hand-held electric mixer with chilled beaters, beat cream mixture, sugar, and vanilla until thick and fluffy. Fold in candy. Scrape into pie shell and spread evenly.

3. *To prepare topping:* In same bowl, using a hand-held electric mixer with same beaters, beat cream with hazelnut chocolate spread until thick and fluffy. Scrape into pie shell. Mound mixture and smooth surface. Sprinkle with grated chocolate and freeze for 6 hours, or until firm. Let sit at room temperature for 10 minutes before serving.

Makes 6 to 8 servings

Note: You can substitute a homemade 8-inch graham cracker pie shell for the commercially prepared one.

If necessary, soften chocolate fudge sauce according to container directions and cool before spreading into pie shell.

· TURTLE ICE CREAM PIE ·

A caramel-pecan mixture and a layer of chocolate fill this luscious pie. For another variation, omit the chocolate layer. Simply fill the pie with the pecan mixture and serve it with Chocolate Sauce (page 132).

CRUST
1½ cups graham cracker crumbs or
   chocolate cookie wafer crumbs

1 tablespoon granulated sugar
6 tablespoons unsalted butter, melted

ICE CREAM FILLING
¼ cup firmly packed brown sugar
2 tablespoons unsalted butter
2 tablespoons light corn syrup
2 tablespoons heavy (whipping) cream

1 teaspoon vanilla extract
⅓ cup chopped pecans
4 cups vanilla or chocolate ice cream,
   softened (see Note)

CHOCOLATE FILLING AND DRIZZLE
3 ounces bittersweet chocolate, finely
   chopped

¼ cup heavy (whipping) cream
1 tablespoon light corn syrup

1. *To prepare crust:* Lightly butter a 9-inch pie plate.

2. In a medium bowl, mix together graham cracker crumbs and sugar. Stir in butter until combined. Using your fingers, firmly and evenly press crumb mixture into bottom and sides of prepared pie plate. Refrigerate pie shell for 10 minutes.

3. *To prepare ice cream filling:* In a small heavy saucepan, over medium heat, stir together sugar, butter, and corn syrup. Heat for 2 to 3 minutes, stirring constantly, until sugar is dissolved and mixture is boiling. Remove pan from heat and whisk in cream and vanilla until blended. Stir in pecans and let mixture stand until it comes to room temperature.

4. Using a rubber spatula, quickly spread half of ice cream into graham cracker crust. Place pie in freezer for 20 to 30 minutes, or until firm.

5. *To prepare chocolate filling and drizzle:* In a medium-size heavy saucepan, over medium-low heat, stir together chocolate, cream, and corn syrup. Stirring constantly with a wooden spoon, heat mixture for 3 to 5 minutes, or until melted and smooth. Remove pan from heat and let stand for 5 minutes.

6. Carefully spoon pecan mixture evenly over ice cream–filled pie. Freeze for 5 to 10 minutes to set. Carefully drizzle about two-thirds of chocolate mixture evenly over pecan mixture. Freeze pie for 3 to 5 minutes to set slightly. Using a rubber spatula, spread remaining 2 cups of softened ice cream over top of pie and return to freezer for 10 to 15 minutes.

7. Using a small spoon, drizzle remaining chocolate mixture over top of pie. Freeze for 6 hours, or until firm.

Makes 6 to 8 servings

Note: For this recipe, soften half the ice cream at a time. You can soften ice cream by placing in refrigerator (not freezer) for 20 to 30 minutes. Or, alternatively, place ice cream in a microwave oven set on MEDIUM for 20-second intervals until softened. Do not allow ice cream to melt.

Quick Chocolate Candies

· CHOCOLATE PRALINE TRUFFLES ·

These truffles take time, but they're actually quite easy to prepare. Plus they make a great hostess or holiday gift.

¹/₄ cup granulated sugar
2 tablespoons water, rum, or bourbon
1 scant cup pecans or walnuts
9 ounces bittersweet chocolate, broken
*   into pieces*

2 tablespoons unsalted butter, at room
*   temperature*
2 tablespoons heavy (whipping) cream, at
*   room temperature*
1 teaspoon vanilla extract
Dash salt

1.   Lightly oil a 10-inch-diameter circle on a baking sheet. In a small heavy saucepan, stir together sugar and water, rum, or bourbon. Cook, over medium heat, stirring constantly, until sugar dissolves. Increase heat to high and bring mixture to a boil. Cook without stirring for approximately 3¹/₂ minutes, or until mixture turns amber and caramelizes. Immediately add nuts and stir to coat with syrup. Immediately scrape mixture onto oiled part of prepared baking sheet. Cool for 20 minutes, or until hardened. Transfer mixture to a cutting board and coarsely chop praline. Finely chop enough praline to make ¹/₃ cup; set aside. Place remainder of praline into container of food processor fitted with a steel blade. Process until praline is very finely chopped.

2.   In a microwave-safe bowl, heat chocolate in a microwave oven on HIGH for 1 to 3 minutes, stirring halfway through cooking, until chocolate is melted (or use a double boiler over hot, not simmering, water). Stir in butter until melted. Stir in cream, vanilla,

and salt until blended. Let mixture cool for 5 minutes. Stir in reserved ⅓ cup chopped praline. Refrigerate chocolate mixture for 30 to 90 minutes, or until firm enough to shape. Shape level tablespoonfuls of chocolate mixture into balls. Refrigerate as needed while shaping chocolate. Roll balls into finely chopped praline to coat. If necessary, refrigerate until firm. Store truffles in an airtight container in refrigerator. Let truffles reach room temperature before serving.

Makes approximately 18 candies

Variation: For a super-quick variation, you can substitute 1 cup finely chopped peanut brittle (about 4½ ounces). Set aside ⅓ cup and place remainder in container of food processor fitted with a steel blade and proceed as directed.

Note: Leftover chopped praline can be served as a topping for ice cream. You can make these candies smaller if desired.

• FAST FUDGE •

Here's an easy recipe for fudge that is extra smooth because it uses cream cheese. The tang of the cream cheese helps keep this fudge from being oversweet.

1 package (8 ounces) cream cheese, at
  room temperature
2 cups semisweet chocolate chips, melted
  and cooled

½ cup chopped walnuts or pecans
1 teaspoon vanilla extract

1. Lightly coat an 8-inch-square baking pan with nonstick vegetable cooking spray.
2. In a large bowl, using a hand-held electric mixer, beat cream cheese just until smooth. Beat in melted chips and vanilla. Using a wooden spoon, stir in nuts.
3. Scrape batter into prepared pan and spread evenly. Cover and refrigerate until firm. Cut into 1-inch squares. Store in an airtight container in refrigerator. Serve chilled or at room temperature.
Makes approximately 64 candies

• GORP CLUSTERS •

Good Old Raisins and Peanuts make a tasty addition to this three-ingredient recipe, with chocolate chips forming the basis of the candies.

1 cup semisweet or milk chocolate
   chips

½ cup dry-roasted peanuts
½ cup raisins

1. In a microwave-safe bowl, heat chips in a microwave oven on HIGH for 1 to 2 minutes, stirring halfway through cooking until chips are melted (or use a double boiler over hot, not simmering, water). Stir in peanuts and raisins until coated with chocolate.

2. Drop mixture by teaspoonfuls onto a wax paper–lined baking sheet and refrigerate until firm. Remove candies from wax paper. Store candies in refrigerator or at cool room temperature.

Makes approximately 24 candies

• MOCHA RUM CARIBBEAN CANDIES •

Hey, Mon, these candies might be sort of ugly, but they taste great. Pass around a platter of these after an island-themed party.

¾ cup raisins
¼ cup dark rum
⅓ cup sweetened flaked coconut

9 ounces coffee-flavored milk or bittersweet
chocolate, melted

1. In a microwave-safe bowl, heat raisins and rum in a microwave oven on HIGH for 1 to 2 minutes, stirring halfway through cooking. Stir in coconut. Stir in chocolate until ingredients are combined.

2. Drop mixture by teaspoonfuls onto a wax paper–lined baking sheet and refrigerate until firm. Remove candies from wax paper. Store candies in refrigerator or at cool room temperature.

Makes approximately 24 candies

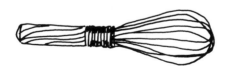

· NONPAREILS ·

An easy-to-make treat, you can make these anytime you have leftover chocolate. This recipe can be doubled.

2 ounces bittersweet chocolate, chopped
1 teaspoon unsalted butter

Approximately 3 to 4 tablespoons candy
sprinkles

In top of a double boiler, over hot, not simmering, water, heat chocolate and butter, stirring until melted. Remove pan from heat (or, in a microwave-safe bowl, heat chocolate and butter on HIGH for 1 to 2 minutes, stirring halfway through cooking until chocolate is melted). Drop chocolate by heaping ½ teaspoonfuls onto a wax paper–lined baking sheet, to form mounds approximately 1 inch in diameter. Spoon a small amount of sprinkles over each chocolate mound to coat surface. Refrigerate to set chocolate. Let candy reach room temperature before serving.

Makes approximately 20 candies

Note: You can make these candies larger if desired. *Suggestion:* Do not tip the baking sheet to remove excess sprinkles until the chocolate is set.

• PEANUT BUTTER CHOCOLATE CHIP DROPS •

These peanut butter and chocolate candies are sure to be kid-pleasers.

*3 ounces white chocolate, coarsely
    chopped*

¹/₃ cup smooth peanut butter
¹/₂ cup milk chocolate chips

1. In top of a double boiler, over hot, not simmering, water, melt white chocolate, stirring occasionally, until smooth (see Note). Remove top part of double boiler from bottom and cool chocolate for about 3 minutes. Stir in peanut butter until blended.
2. Refrigerate for approximately 10 minutes, or until mixture starts to mound. Stir in chips. Drop by heaping teaspoonfuls onto a wax paper–lined baking sheet. Refrigerate for 15 minutes, or until firm. Let candies sit at room temperature for 5 minutes before serving.

Makes approximately 14 candies

Note: You can also spoon level tablespoonfuls of peanut butter mixture into 2-inch-diameter or smaller paper baking cups. The yield will vary depending on size of candies.

To melt white chocolate in a microwave oven, in a microwave-safe bowl, heat chocolate on HIGH for 1 to 3 minutes, stirring halfway through cooking, until chocolate is melted.

· WHITE CHOCOLATE MOCHA CANDIES ·

White chocolate and mocha combine to create these easy-to-make, yet elegant candies.

3 ounces white chocolate, coarsely chopped
¼ cup heavy (whipping) cream, divided

2 tablespoons chopped, slivered, blanched almonds, toasted
3 ounces coffee-flavored chocolate, coarsely chopped

1.   In top of double boiler, over hot, not simmering, water, melt white chocolate and 2 tablespoons cream, stirring occasionally until smooth (see Note). Stir in nuts. Divide mixture evenly among twelve 2-inch paper baking cups.

2.   Add coffee-flavored chocolate and remaining 2 tablespoons of cream to top of double boiler, melt over hot, not simmering, water, stirring occasionally until smooth. Pour mixture over white chocolate in baking cups. Chill for 1 hour, or until firm. Remove candies from baking cups and let sit at room temperature for 5 minutes before serving.

Makes approximately 12 candies

Note: To melt chocolate in a microwave oven, in a microwave-safe bowl, heat chocolate on HIGH for 1 to 3 minutes, stirring halfway through cooking, until chocolate is melted.

· WHITE CHOCOLATE GRANOLA CLUSTERS ·

These easy-to-make candies feature a delicious combination of tart dried fruit, sweet white chocolate, and crunchy granola. You can experiment by trying your own combinations, such as dried pineapple and macadamia nuts.

*6 ounces white chocolate, coarsely
    chopped*
*3/4 cup granola without raisins (low-fat
    or regular variety)*

*1/2 cup coarsely chopped dried cranberries,
    dried tart cherries, or dried apricots (see
    Note)*

1. In top of a double boiler, over hot, not simmering, water, melt chocolate, stirring occasionally, until smooth (see Note). Remove top part of double boiler from bottom and cool chocolate for 5 minutes. Stir in granola and cranberries.

2. Drop by heaping tablespoonfuls onto a wax paper–lined baking sheet. Refrigerate for 30 minutes, or until set. Let candies sit at room temperature for 5 minutes before serving.

Makes approximately 14 candies

Note: Dried cranberries and cherries are often available in gourmet food stores, or can be ordered by mail (page 12).

To melt white chocolate in a microwave oven, in a microwave-safe bowl, heat chocolate on HIGH for 1 to 3 minutes, stirring halfway through cooking, until chocolate is melted.

Quick Chocolate Beverages, Sauces, and Toppings

• CHOCOLATE BANANA SHAKE •

The first time Leslie tested this recipe, plastic wrap from the frozen bananas was inadvertently processed in the blender with the shake. When her husband Lowell tasted the shake he said it had a strange texture. Leslie insisted it must be flecks of frozen banana and asked him to taste it again. After he almost choked, Leslie finally tasted it and discovered the problem. Lowell knew that bananas were somewhat high in fiber—but not **that** high.

Keep frozen bananas on hand so you can prepare this treat anytime—just be sure to remove the wrapper.

¾ cup milk, well chilled
3 tablespoons chocolate syrup
½ teaspoon vanilla extract

1 large ripe banana, peeled, cut up, and
frozen in an airtight container or plastic
wrap

In a blender container, combine all ingredients and process until smooth. Serve immediately.

(Yield: approximately 1⅔ cups) Makes 1 to 2 servings

• CHOCOLATE MALT •

An old-fashioned soda fountain treat you can make at home. For best results, first place all the ingredients in blender container *except* the ice cream. Measure out ice cream, add to container, blend, and serve immediately.

3/4 cup milk, well chilled
1 tablespoon malted milk powder
   (original flavor or chocolate)

1 tablespoon chocolate syrup
1/2 teaspoon vanilla extract
1 1/2 cups chocolate ice cream

In a blender container, combine all ingredients and process until smooth.
(*Yield: approximately 1 3/4 cups*) *Makes 1 to 2 servings*

Note: Substitute 3 tablespoons of commercially-prepared chocolate malt syrup for the malted milk powder and chocolate syrup. Proceed as directed.

· CHOCOLATE MARSHMALLOW TOPPING ·

Try this fun topping on your favorite ice cream.

1½ cups miniature marshmallows
3 ounces bittersweet chocolate, chopped

½ cup heavy (whipping) cream
½ teaspoon vanilla extract

In top of a double boiler, over hot, not simmering, water, combine marshmallows, chocolate, and cream. Cook, stirring often, until blended. Remove top of double boiler from heat, stir in vanilla. Allow mixture to cool for 10 minutes before serving. Store sauce in an airtight container in refrigerator.

Makes approximately 1 cup

Note: To reheat topping, place in microwave-safe container and microwave on MEDIUM for 30 to 60 seconds (depending on amount of topping) until melted. Let cool to pouring consistency before serving.

• CHOCOLATE SAUCE •

A rich chocolate sauce that tastes great on ice cream, as well as cakes. Be sure to try the Chocolate Malt and Mocha Sauce variations, too.

4 ounces bittersweet chocolate, chopped
1 tablespoon unsalted butter
2 teaspoons light corn syrup

½ cup heavy (whipping) cream
1 tablespoon confectioners' sugar
½ teaspoon vanilla extract

In top of a double boiler, over hot, not simmering, water, melt chocolate and butter, stirring often, until smooth. Stir in corn syrup until blended. Stir in cream and sugar. Remove top of double boiler from heat, stir in vanilla. Allow mixture to cool for 10 minutes before serving. Store sauce in an airtight container in refrigerator.

Makes approximately 1 cup

Note: To reheat sauce, place in microwave-safe container and microwave on MEDIUM for 30 to 60 seconds (depending on amount of chocolate sauce) until melted. Let cool to pouring consistency before serving.

For Chocolate Malt Sauce: Stir 3 tablespoons malted milk powder (original flavor) into cream until dissolved and proceed as directed.

For Mocha Sauce: Stir 1 teaspoon instant espresso powder into cream until dissolved and proceed as directed.

• CHOCOLATY ORANGE SHAKE •

A classic combination for adults only.

1½ cups chocolate ice cream
½ cup milk, well-chilled
2 to 3 tablespoons orange-flavored
    liqueur, such as Cointreau or Grand
    Marnier

1 tablespoon chocolate syrup (commercially
    prepared, or homemade, page 139)

In a blender container, combine all ingredients and process until smooth.
(*Yield: approximately 1¾ cups*) *Makes 1 to 2 servings*

• CLASSIC CHOCOLATE SHAKE •

Store glasses in the freezer so you'll always have frosted glasses on hand for this and other cold beverages. Add more milk to this recipe for a thinner shake.

1 cup chocolate ice cream
¼ cup milk, well chilled

In a blender container, combine all ingredients and process until smooth. Pour into a chilled glass and serve.
Makes 1 serving

• DOUBLE ICED MOCHA COFFEE •

Freeze leftover coffee in ice cube trays to have on hand so you can make this drink anytime.

½ cup milk, well chilled
¼ cup iced coffee
2 tablespoons commercially prepared
  chocolate syrup (or homemade,
  page 139)

4 "iced coffee" ice cubes (see Note)
Sugar or sweetener to taste

In a blender container, combine all ingredients and process until almost smooth. Serve immediately.

(Yield: approximately 1½ cups) Makes 1 to 2 servings

Note: To make "iced coffee" ice cubes, fill an ice cube tray with cooled coffee and freeze until firm.

• EGG CREAM •

A chocolate egg cream is a fizzy soda fountain drink native to New York City. In spite of its name, it does not contain eggs or cream. It is best made with seltzer that is dispensed from an old-fashioned siphon bottle. Use brand-new seltzer to get the optimum amount of fizz.

1 cup milk, well chilled
3 tablespoons chocolate syrup, homemade
(page 139) or store-bought

½ to ¾ cup seltzer, well chilled

1. Place a large glass in sink. Pour milk and chocolate syrup into glass and stir to combine.
2. Pour seltzer into glass until there is a foamy head.
Makes 1 serving

Variation: For an Egg Cream Supreme, add a scoop of vanilla, chocolate, or coffee ice cream.

· ICED MOCHA COFFEE ·

A delicious drink for hot summer days. You may need to adjust the proportion of ingredients to your own taste.

1 cup iced coffee
½ cup milk, or to taste
2 tablespoons commercially prepared
chocolate syrup, or to taste

2 to 3 ice cubes
Sugar or sweetener to taste

In a blender container, combine all ingredients and process until almost smooth. Serve immediately.

(Yield: approximately 1½ cups) Makes 1 to 2 servings

Note: Commercially prepared chocolate milk can be substituted for the milk and chocolate syrup.

• MEXICAN HOT CHOCOLATE •

While the classic recipe for Mexican hot chocolate calls for ground almonds, here's a version that uses almond extract and is smoother in texture. To keep the beverage toasty warm, run the mug under hot water before filling with the hot chocolate.

2 teaspoons unsweetened cocoa powder
1 tablespoon granulated sugar
Dash ground cinnamon
Approximately 1 cup milk

¹/₈ teaspoon vanilla extract
Scant ¹/₈ teaspoon almond extract
Cinnamon stick, for garnish (optional)

In a 1-cup microwave-safe measuring cup, stir together cocoa powder, sugar, and cinnamon. Add 2 teaspoons of milk and stir until smooth. Fill cup to 1-cup mark with remaining milk and stir. Heat in a microwave oven on **HIGH** for 1 to 2 minutes, or until hot. Stir in vanilla and almond extracts until combined. Serve in a warm mug. Add a cinnamon stick for garnish, if desired.

Makes 1 serving

· MOCHA HAZELNUT SHAKE ·

A sophisticated flavor combination for adults only.

1/3 cup milk, well-chilled
2 tablespoons hazelnut chocolate spread
  (such as Nutella)

1 1/2 cups coffee ice cream
2 tablespoons hazelnut-flavored liqueur

In a blender container, combine milk and hazelnut chocolate spread; process until smooth. Add remaining ingredients and process until smooth.

(Yield: approximately 1 2/3 cups) Makes 1 to 2 servings

· ADULT AFTER-DINNER MINT SHAKE ·

Here's a beverage that's perfect as a refreshing finale after dinner.

1 1/2 cups chocolate ice cream
1/3 cup milk, well chilled

2 tablespoons white crème de menthe

In a blender container, combine all ingredients and process until smooth. Pour into chilled glasses and serve.

(Yield: approximately 1 1/3 cups) Makes 2 servings

· OLD-FASHIONED CHOCOLATE SYRUP ·

Here's a homemade version of chocolate syrup. Store it in a squeeze bottle in your refrigerator to flavor beverages and to squirt over the top of ice cream and other desserts.

½ cup light corn syrup
¼ cup water
⅓ cup unsweetened cocoa powder

⅓ cup granulated sugar
1 teaspoon vanilla extract

In a small heavy saucepan, stir together corn syrup, water, cocoa powder, and sugar. Cook over high heat, stirring constantly, until mixture comes to a boil. Boil, stirring constantly, for 1 minute. Remove pan from heat. Stir in vanilla. Cool and store syrup in an airtight container in refrigerator for up to 10 days.

Makes approximately ¾ cup

· PEANUTTY CHOCOLATE SHAKE ·

A kid-pleasing snack you can whip up in a flash. Adjust the peanut flavor to your taste.

1½ cups chocolate ice cream
⅔ cup milk, well chilled
1½ to 2 tablespoons creamy peanut
  butter, or more to taste

½ teaspoon vanilla extract (optional)

In a blender container, combine all ingredients and process until smooth.
(*Yield: approximately 1¾ cups*) *Makes 1 to 2 servings*

• SWISS HOT CHOCOLATE •

This super-rich hot drink is packed with chocolate flavor from melted Swiss chocolate.

2 ounces Swiss dark chocolate, coarsely
 chopped

¾ cup milk
⅛ teaspoon vanilla

In a 1-cup microwave-safe measuring cup, heat chocolate in a microwave oven on HIGH for 1 to 2 minutes, stirring halfway through cooking until chocolate is melted. Gradually whisk in milk until combined. Return cup to microwave oven and heat on HIGH for 30 to 60 seconds, or until mixture is heated through. Stir in vanilla.

Makes 1 serving

· WET WALNUT CHOCOLATE CHIP TOPPING ·

Here's a syrupy topping that is packed full of walnuts and chocolate chips. It's great over ice cream. For a super treat, place a scoop of ice cream on a waffle and top with a generous spoonful of this sauce.

³/₄ cup firmly packed brown sugar
¹/₂ cup water
¹/₄ cup light corn syrup

2 teaspoons vanilla extract
¹/₂ cup chopped walnuts or pecans
¹/₃ cup miniature semisweet chocolate chips

In a heavy saucepan, stir together sugar, water, and syrup. Cook over medium heat, stirring constantly with a wooden spoon, until sugar is dissolved. Increase heat to medium-high and bring mixture to a boil. Boil, **without stirring**, for 3 minutes. Stir to see if mixture is slightly syrupy. If it's not, boil for 1 to 2 minutes longer. Remove pan from heat. Stir in vanilla. Stir in nuts. Cool to room temperature and stir in chips.

Makes approximately 1³/₄ cups

Index